WISDOM OF THOTH
THE ASTRAL PLANE
AND THE PLEROMA OF
THE GODS

PANTHEON OF AETERNAM

authorHOUSE®

AuthorHouse™ UK
1663 Liberty Drive
Bloomington, IN 47403 USA
www.authorhouse.co.uk
Phone: UK TFN: 0800 0148641 (Toll Free inside the UK)
        UK Local: (02) 0369 56322 (+44 20 3695 6322 from outside the UK)

Published by AuthorHouse 01/12/2023

ISBN: 978-1-7283-7993-7 (sc)
ISBN: 978-1-7283-7992-0 (e)

Print information available on the last page.

Any people depicted in stock imagery provided by Getty Images are models,
and such images are being used for illustrative purposes only.
Certain stock imagery © Getty Images.

This book is printed on acid-free paper.

Because of the dynamic nature of the Internet, any web addresses or links contained in
this book may have changed since publication and may no longer be valid. The views
expressed in this work are solely those of the author and do not necessarily reflect the
views of the publisher, and the publisher hereby disclaims any responsibility for them.

CONTENTS

ACKNOWLEDGEMENT

We would like to express the deepest gratitude to all our order members, students, friends, and supporters of our work who have helped us spread the teachings of the gods and bring light, wisdom and healing to Earth. We are a community of light and we are here to support humanity, experience their true power, purpose and path, connect to their whole being and their astral existence.

Furthermore, we would like to thank the readers of this book and all of you who continue to support our work. We are confident that our book "Wisdom of Thoth - The Astral plane and the Pleroma of Gods" will be a catalyst of truth regarding the creation of the astral plane with all its subplanes and the pleroma of the gods, the cosmic laws, the powerful creative forces of the cosmos, the growth and transformation processes in the astral plane, Earth's ability to receive growth from the astral plane and the ability of human beings to connect to the astral plane and experience cosmic growth in their Earth body.

PREFACE

We are very proud to present this book to you as it is the most powerful and truthful account of cosmic creation and guides humanity to experience their birthplace, the astral plane. This book will teach you about the creation of the divine and cosmic light created by the intention of the source and their unique purpose to create a vast multi-organism, the astral plane, and support its purpose to constantly grow and transform.

The cosmic wisdom that is shared in this book will reconnect you to your astral body and the great cosmic powers that have created it. If you are aware of your whole being including your astral body, your higher self and your creation code then you can experience life in different realms and you can bring high wisdom to your third-dimensional reality. The purpose of all human beings is to connect to the cosmos, experience high growth and transmit cosmic light to Earth and her creation.

The astral plane is the energy space where all life is created. It is a complex electromagnetic field and its energy occupies the greatest part of cosmic creation. It is an enormous, multidimensional energy space of transformation whose starting point is its core. The astral core and the cosmic light are part of the source's being, they exist and grow in unity. The law of unity is a fundamental truth that supports the design of all living beings so the microcosm can continue to grow and transform and the macrocosm can constantly expand in a limitless pool of opportunities that can be transferred to all living beings and all life.

The expansion of the astral core created the astral plane with its many sub-planes of various energetic structures. Unity and growth are two powerful cosmic laws that work together for life to continue to flow in the astral plane. The growth and transformation of light depend on its ability to connect to energy points and maintain life in them as well as support the creation of new life and the expansion of the astral plane. Creating unique astral beings that have wonderful abilities to grow, receive the light and exist in unity with all creation, supports the creative abilities of the light to become a powerful creator.

In this book, you will read about the creation of cosmic and divine light and what was their purpose in the creation of the astral plane. The unity of the divine and cosmic light supported the bond between the source and its cosmic creation and this is how life was maintained and grew in the astral plane. The cosmic light is a pure and powerful cosmic force that creates life in all planes and the divine light is a tool of precision that supports cosmic laws, transformations, movement, growth and connection between all beings and planes.

Astral beings are created by cosmic light and divine light and are part of energy fields that support the expansion of the astral plane and the creation of sub-planes. The purpose of their existence is to support the flow of energy in the astral plane and the creation of growth opportunities for all living beings. Astral beings can achieve this by following cosmic laws and experiencing life as powerful receivers and transmitters of light.

In this book you will read about Earth's connection with the astral plane, reincarnation, transition to the astral plane after the end of a life cycle on Earth and how human beings stay connected to their astral body and experience astral growth as Earth's multidimensional beings.

The invaluable cosmic wisdom that is offered in this book includes teachings communicated to the messengers of the Pantheon of Aeternam, Barbara, and Robbert-jan Rozenkruis by the Light of Thoth. They have been instructed by Thoth to receive these unique teachings and make them available to everyone who is an open channel and wants to connect to truth and cosmic wisdom. There is no secret knowledge to be kept for the selected few. All wisdom is revealed to all who are interested in becoming truth. They do not teach dogma, philosophy, or other man-made theories. They teach ageless wisdom and cosmic truth is given to us by the High Gods of the pleroma.

PANTHEON OF AETERNAM

GOD THOTH

They want to inform people about the creation of the astral plane and cosmic creation that links all creation in all planes. The teachings of the gods will help humanity reconnect to the cosmic seed in them and experience life as a multidimensional being that is in constant unity and growth with the light of the astral plane and the source. Earth's golden era was the result of her connection with her astral body, being able to receive and transmit light and experience cosmic abundance. We are all connected to cosmic creation; this is our starting point where all questions can be answered and all wisdom is shared to assist evolution. We are all connected to the eternal growth of the astral plane and this is the journey that is offered to the readers of this book.

The process of communication between the gods and the messengers cannot be explained or described; it is a cosmic process that is supported by Earth and cosmic energies. They received this gift in order to assist the gods to communicate and awakening humanity during this crucial time in Earth's history.

The messengers don't try to explain the communication process; they are very grateful that they were chosen and have made this work the focus of their lives. The teachings presented in this book have not been altered or edited. They are faithful accounts of the wisdom of the gods.

For more information about the Pantheon of Aeternam you can visit our website.
http://pantheonofaeternam.com

The order Pantheon of Aeternam is open to all. There is no secret knowledge to be kept for the selected few; instead, all wisdom should be revealed to all who are interested in becoming the truth. This is an important time and we all have to support Earth and restore her to the most graceful expression of herself, her golden age. There is a divine plan and a high project of creation that involves humanity and Earth experiencing cosmic growth. Thoth's teachings are spreading to Earth in order to restore truth, high light, and bring growth for all human beings and their mother Earth. Humanity and Earth are called to connect and follow the divine plan and common purpose. The order Pantheon of Aeternam is open to all. There is no secret knowledge to be kept for the selected few; instead, all wisdom should be revealed to all who are interested in becoming the truth. This is an important time and we all have to support Earth and restore her to the most graceful expression of herself, her golden age.

What is the Pantheon of Aeternam?

In 2014, Barbara and Robbert-jan Rozenkruis came together and planted the first seeds for the creation of the Pantheon of Aeternam community. Their connection was so powerful that instantly guided them to the life purpose that has supported their project and offered great healing to both of them and thousands of people who connect to their work.

Robbert-jan and Barbara are very different: come from different backgrounds, had different experiences and lived in different countries but they share a common path. The light that they shared when they first met created a new life for both of them and a common purpose. Their life was based on love, deep connection, healing, openness, truth, gratitude and the discovery of their special gifts and path.

When they first met they had communication with Christian Rosencreutz. The messages they received guided them to overcome different obstacles and start building their life together. They received teachings and guidance that helped them heal, connect to their whole being, and open up to cosmic light of Thoth. Their process of communication with Thoth is instant and effortless. Barbara is experiencing a deep state of peace, she is aware of her whole being and she opens up to the Earth and the cosmos to receive the cosmic guidance. All these practices happen simultaneously and instantly and Barbara is able to receive and share not only messages but also light and energy that produces these messages.

They do not perform any rituals, they are not restricted to have this communication only on certain times/days at a special location or at a specific high energy spot. They do not use crystals, sounds, symbols, or plant medicine. They are a pure channel of divine energy and the connection is instant, direct, and can take place any time, whenever they want to offer healing and light to Earth and humanity.

They have received thousands of teachings, some of which are published in their books "Fountain Source of High Wisdom-Sacred Book of Thoth", "Wisdom of Thoth", Sacred Book of Earth, and many others they share with members of their community for healing purposes and cosmic expansion. The purpose of this gift is to awaken humanity to their true power to grow with Earth as multidimensional beings; to experience their purpose which is collective purification and growth.

Robert-jan and Barbara are very grateful that they were chosen to carry this gift and they have made this work the focus of their lives. When they first started to communicate with the Light of Thoth they had profound experiences that led to an awakening. The Light created a sacred place in them, an expansive energy field, and then were able to connect to their own light, initiating purification and connection to their true self.

When you connect to your true self, your life transforms into an open path of limitless growth and transformation. This is how you can become the creator of your own life and purify your whole being from the distortion that exists on Earth. The light of the cosmos is a great guide and is supporting humanity and Earth to find their way back to the Golden Age. Human beings and Earth have a collective purpose and are able to receive the light and grow in unity.

The physical body is created by Earth and is aware of our purpose and divine plan. In other words, we are all here as a gift to Earth, supporting Earth's growth. We exist in unity with Earth and her creation and this is how we grow. Thoth's teachings are cosmic wisdom and teach humanity about cosmic laws, Earth's creation and purpose, enlightenment, healing, distortion on Earth, reincarnation, the astral plane, the pleroma, and much more.

It is important that we all become perfect receivers and transmitters of light, we all grow together, exist in unity, and be part of the divine plan. Robert-jan and Barbara want to teach humanity a life of unity and effortless growth and the teachings that they share will help people purify from all imbalances, connect to their whole being, experience their path, and be able to exist in unity with Earth and the cosmos. Their high duty is to connect humanity with Earth and the cosmos; clear all illusion and distortion and restore the high vibrational LIGHT that once existed on Earth during the golden era.

Human beings are coming to Earth having a purpose and a divine plan, unique abilities leading to an effortless life of receiving and transmitting LIGHT, growth, and transformation. The truth in you is not a belief or an idea; it is a living being that can connect you with Earth and her high light that is her golden era as well as the infinite cosmic growth. When human beings understand and experience these connections they will enter a greater space of growth. Limitations/fears/separation can affect the mind and the physical body when a being is confused, disconnected from truth, and unaware of their purpose in this lifetime. When human beings are in this state they are powerless against distortion. Life on Earth becomes a traumatic experience and the mind focuses on the pain. Human beings have the ability to share, connect, and grow with others; if your mind is affected by distortion you can only spread distortion. People should experience freedom. You are free to love yourself and connect to Earthly and cosmic nourishment, experience healing, transformation, and growth.

There are many gifts that are stored in you: your light, truth, pure intention, path, purpose, inner calling can help you experience freedom. You are free to connect to Earth, receive nourishment, heal, and grow. The Pantheon of Aeternam was created to accomplish a special duty: to purify humanity and support the coming of a new golden era on Earth. With Thoth's teachings, Barbara and Robbert-jan want to restore truth and freedom and bring high growth to all human beings and the planet. Human beings need to purify from distortion that breeds illusion, artificiality, and fragmentation. We have to learn to exist in a space of unity; act with purity and focus on growth.

Disconnecting from illusionary thoughts, expectations, and ideals allow healing to enter your being. This can be achieved when people go through a process of purification and transformation. Purification is an exercise of knowing, healing, and empowerment and you should follow it. Look at your imbalances with acceptance. Learn to be an observer of your own actions and be aware of their impact. Connect to your being, quieten your mind, disconnect from the persona. Truth is your only tool to high wisdom. In this space of truth, you are called to purify yourself and allow healing to reach your imbalances. Open to the light of the cosmos that can heal you and nourish you. Your connection to the light will purify and bring balance to you. By connecting to the cosmic light, knowing yourself, and having pure intention, you are transforming and moving closer to your higher self. Purification is a unique self-healing process and includes the study and practice of observation, creating a space of peace, connecting to your whole being, and allowing the energies of the cosmos and Earth to enter your body and start your healing process. When people practice purification they experience intense healing that purifies them from imbalances, trauma, and fear patterns. Life can become an effortless flow of growth when people are free to follow their path.

Pantheon of Aeternam has published three more books that can be used as a guide to help you discover cosmic truths shared by Thoth and start your healing process. The first book "Fountain Source of High Wisdom-Sacred Book of Thoth" was published in February 2015. In this book, there are more than 200 teachings, a complete vocabulary section plus extra teaching material including more than forty questions and answers. The teachings in this book share light on many topics including the creation of Earth, Earth races, Cosmic creation, Astral plane, Higher self, Creation code, Reincarnation, Cosmic laws, Growth, Purpose, Cosmic Healing, Love, Manipulation on Earth, Living the illusion, Transformation of a physical being, The Connection between Physical and Astral Body, True Seekers of Wisdom in Ancient Times, Hollow of the Earth, Conscious Living and the ideal State of Humanity. For more information about our book, you can visit our website: http://pantheonofaeternam.co.uk/fountain-source-of-high-wisdom-sacred-book-of-tho th.html

Pantheon of Aeternam's second book has the title "Wisdom of Thoth" and was published in February 2019. This book was created to help you connect to truth and express it in your everyday life and creative process. It contains more than 300 pages of cosmic wisdom and focuses on Healing, Purification, Connecting to Earth's energies, Growth, Physical body and Energy field, Dealing with imbalances, Observing patterns, Illusion-Fear-Limitation, Building communities of truth, Guides, Life on other planets, Cosmic creation, Astral Growth, Source, and many more. Read more about this book on the Pantheon of Aeternam's website: http://pantheonofaeternam.co.uk/books.html#wisdomofthoth

Pantheon of Aeternam' third book has the title "Sacred Book of Earth" and was published in 2021. It is the most powerful and truthful account of Earth's creation and sets the starting point for humanity to journey back to Earth of the golden era, experience her powerful creative powers, gifts, purpose, path and bring this high point of growth in their present moment. The cosmic wisdom that is shared in this book will take you to a time when physicality did not exist. The only plane where all life was created, was the astral plane. This book will show you how and why Earth's golden era came to an end. You will read about the transformations that Earth and other planets had to experience during these turbulent times and how this affected their creation.

If you wish to order any of our books you can contact us by email: pantheonofaeternam@gmail.com

PANTHEON OF AETERNAM

Chapter I

You are able to receive the light from the astral plane to your physical reality and you are able to create with it. At the end of a life cycle, your physical body returns to Earth and you gradually return to the astral plane. You already exist in the astral plane and you have to go through a process of purification and detachment from the persona and imbalances that were created during your reincarnation.

Introduction

I want people to wake up to the truth and realise that their world is a fantasy. Their power is taken away and the ability to communicate with the divine is weak, being confused with new spirituality and relevant philosophies and practices. There is a simple way to be enlightened and this means that you will be able to receive your first lesson in cosmic truth when you are true to yourself. It seems like a simple task but for many people on Earth is one of the greatest challenges.

Open your eyes and see that everything around you is false, artificial, distorted and has no true purpose. You are offered choices that are limitations, gateways to diversions and mazes of confusion. Some people may think that they have no choice but to accept the illusion in order to survive. I say that you are all free to grow and transform and your life choices should reflect the greatness and clarity of your path.

Do not give your power away because if you do you also give away your purpose. I want to see the people of Earth naked without the old garments, standing as true beings to receive grace and follow their path. These are the beings that will connect to the gods and reach the Pleroma.

Wisdom of Thoth: The purpose of all human beings

Human beings are constantly affected by distortion and this is demonstrated in the way they think, act and live their lives. Even when they connect to their own truth after a deep purification process they may still go on a diversion looking for truth elsewhere.

Sometimes people blame this on their everyday challenges such as finances, family/relationships, being stuck or confused as well as not having enough support to overcome these challenges.

It is the purpose of all human beings to transform their challenges into opportunities and experience a life of growth. Instead, people are supporting these challenges to become black holes and they fall into a state of absolute weakness and confusion. You can help yourself by focusing on growth instead of the obstacle and strengthening your ability to grow.

You are going to love your whole being when you connect to the seed of truth in you. If you can not see it ask yourself this question: What makes me truly happy? Describe a moment of perfect bliss. If you have to give to others the most precious part of your being, what will this be? These questions can be your guide to your truth and help you focus on growth and opportunities for transformation. Focus on the beauty of your being; it will help you grow.

Introduction

There are many teachers who try to reassure their followers that enlightenment is available to all even if their focus is to maintain a clear division between the enlightened teacher and his/hers students who are desperately trying to experience enlightenment, often unsuccessfully. I have said before that Earth is a land of multiple layers of distortion. Living in a state of distortion you live in a constant illusion where there is no growth. Furthermore, the ruling classes that try to control and manipulate human minds, have the perfect foundation for building and strengthening their control mechanisms. Manipulation and distortion support and strengthen each other.

In order to reach the state of truth you have to question yourself: what is real in my life; what brings me pure happiness and growth; what is my true purpose and what do I need to do to fulfil my purpose? These are the questions that you have to ask yourself if you wish to have a happy life and wake up to your true potential. It is natural that when you grow and you follow your true path you are euphoric because your vibration rises, you are experiencing light in your being and you are there supporting others to get on their path and experience their light.

Wisdom of Thoth: Human beings and enlightenment

Human beings have been thinking about enlightenment for thousands of years. For many people, enlightenment is the messiah sitting at the top of the pyramid, throwing the ropes to the followers, and by holding these ropes, they can climb up on a pyramid that they cannot experience.

Human beings are waiting for somebody to save them. They may be curious, full of questions about everything around them, looking for answers and the high wisdom of the enlightened but they never see their being, their truth, or their path.

Human beings have to realize that the messiah archetype is the garment of a ruler who is going to support their ability to fantasize about standing at the top of the pyramid and controlling all human beings that standing on the base. Establishing an unshakable authority is the intention of this archetype; waking up and experiencing truth is seen as a "diversion".

It is also interesting that the self-proclaimed enlightened masters that walked on Earth repeatedly use the pyramid structure to convince and receive attention. At the moment people are very attracted not only to following these masters but also to becoming one. Humanity is experiencing multiple layers of confusion. When human beings follow distortion they create a distorted reality. Do not look at pyramids for enlightenment and success; the depth of your being is your true treasure. Observe yourself at this present moment! Building pyramids is not a path of truth.

Introduction

Illusion is easily accepted by human beings when they remain passive and allow others to spoon-feed them any false reality. They enjoy when they have to do nothing, just follow mechanical patterns, choices and opportunities which are all illusionary. Humans are an easy target for those who create illusions; they are the type of consumers who will buy everything at any price. There is a reason for that: it is their trauma and the fear of survival that has taken away the clarity.

Human beings have blocked high energies to grow in them because they are focusing on the five senses-stimulation and other artificial mind structures. They never question illusionary reality or false beliefs and passively follow the social criteria of success and happiness.

Wisdom of Thoth: Trends

Trends, trends, trends! When will human beings stop following the illusion that has countless faces and come back to the truth of their existence? The so-called awakened ones are following the latest trends and philosophies created by illusionary minds. The awakened ones can often look for power and financial rewards and consciously seek to experience the power of the social pyramid.

The awakened ones are looking for hope but they are still very afraid deep inside them because what they seek and what they are do not follow the same path. The awakened ones are people's pleasers and they often find it necessary to satisfy people's egos and artificial needs. This is happening because the awakened is not awake.

There are people on Earth who experience the illusion of awakening and knowingly or not, create rivers of illusion and throw into these rivers all people who are looking for truth but still wearing a blindfold. Humanity has to escape this new disease, following the awakened and diving more and more into the confusion and limitation. Stand up and observe yourselves, connect to Earth and accept her as a mother. Dive into your being and see the true power of growth in you. Without clarity, you will be a prisoner of illusion.

Introduction

There are humans that believe that growth in the cosmos is divided into different dimensions. There are human beings who believe that Earth is currently experiencing the third dimension but will soon ascend to the fourth and fifth dimensions. As one ascends beyond the 5th dimension, one can activate their spiritual gifts and is able to be healed and experience a multi-dimensional reality. People on Earth are getting ready to ascend. Some feel they have already ascended and are able to demonstrate supernatural powers and create miracles. Is this the true purpose of humanity and Earth?

Wisdom of Thoth: Dimensions and ascension

There are human beings who are wondering about life on other planes and were given some information that has become a belief, that life is divided into universes and dimensions.

There are human beings who believe that Earth is currently experiencing the third dimension but will soon ascend to the fourth and fifth dimensions. This will allow Earth to have higher consciousness and be free from the limitations of physicality.

Furthermore, there are planets and star systems that experience the sixth, and seventh dimensions already and can support Earth to expand and grow into these higher levels of consciousness.

Do not feed your mind with divisions and separations. Do not see the cosmos as a pyramid structure where living beings have to fight and struggle to move to the next level. There is no competition between living beings. Human beings are not created to fit a pyramid scheme that divides them into superior and inferior. All living beings carry light, truth, purpose, unique abilities and they are constantly supported by powerful creative forces. They can all experience a path of abundance and countless opportunities for growth.

When you connect to your whole existence and you are able to reach your core, you will discover that all beings are flowing towards the unified cosmic growth that is supported by cosmic and divine light. The physical plane still exists because it is supported by astral growth and cosmic laws.

The empowerment that all living beings are experiencing in this present moment brings them closer to the light of the source in a process of constant expansion. The pyramid structure dimension belief tries to define growth therefore it creates illusionary obstacles and hardship for the ones who want to reach higher levels of consciousness. If you see life as a flow, growth is constant and unity becomes reality.

Introduction

Teachings are coming down from the High Source to the Gods and masters; they are falling on Earth to the ones who have ears and eyes, clarity and courage to dedicate their lives to this godly service. We have the ability to transform ourselves. We were given this ability by our Source. Masters who can experience this, can create everything that can help them fulfil their purpose. These masters have a clear and pure intention and they are able to see their path and all opportunities to help them experience cosmic abundance. When you master clarity with your whole being you allow yourself to grow in the light, sharing the light.

Wisdom of Thoth: Seek clarity

There are many beings on Earth who are longing to achieve clarity, and connect to their true purpose, but they are entangled in the web of illusion and limitation.

You won't experience clarity if you are not open to connecting to it. Try to answer a simple question with as much clarity as you can. Then listen to your answer, and try to connect your answer with your being.

Many of you will realize that your answers and your statements are often influenced by many external factors. Learn to answer; connect to your true self and this will give you the wisdom you seek. Let's go back to my first question: where do you see yourself in the different stages of evolution? What do you do in order to receive the light and continue with your growth and what are the earthly actions that can help you to achieve that or block your way?

Beings who want to receive the light should be concerned about their light and what they are able to create with it. I want to see more people looking at these questions and answering them with clarity and truth. This is your assignment for those who are seeking enlightenment.

Introduction

Facing yourself with honesty and compassion will help you realize that it is not difficult to step away from illusion. You can empower yourself and raise your vibration if you allow truth to rule your mind and clarity to guide your actions.

When you restore balance in yourself, you will experience full satisfaction at all levels of your existence. When all parts of yourself are able to communicate and harmonize with each other; when you are able to connect to Earth's energies and the astral plane; when you are a receiver and transmitter of high light and you are able to support others then you have achieved the high goal which is accelerated growth. This is available to all beings and it is necessary for all beings to achieve this high goal.

Wisdom of Thoth: Deep impurities within the being

When humans experience upheaval in the mind and their environments such as negativity, fear, weakness and confusion, they are called to enter into their being and experience peace.

They are called to disconnect from artificial realities that are affecting the mind and go into the emptiness of the state of peace. This will lead them to purification, releasing impurities and reconnecting to their truth.

What happens when human beings can not reach their state of peace not because of turbulence coming from their environment but because it is an experience that is affecting parts of their being constantly? When humans experience this, they have created blocks to separate them from their truth. They have allowed distortion from their environment to become a chronic disease and are blocking the route to peace.

These people are going to need great support to overcome these challenges. They will need to disconnect from others and an environment that carries heavily distorted energies. They will have to live in a natural location close to Earth, nourish themselves with healthy food and focus on their wellbeing. They should experience life connecting to the light of the cosmos and the powerful energies of the Earth. There is something more that they have to do: to observe themselves and restore clarity. The confusion in them is their biggest enemy. It supports their illusionary needs, their fears, blocks and obstacles. Clarity will teach you to overcome distortion and remain in a peaceful state.

Introduction

When your vibration rises and your consciousness expands, you will be able to understand the different planes and the different forms of life that exist in multiple dimensions and universes. You will experience the light travelling through all planes and uniting all energy fields and connection points in the cosmos. All beings have the ability to expand and grow because of cosmic unity. You will realise then that all beings can transform and raise their vibration and they are in a process of constant growth. By growing, you are able to produce more light and also transmit more light to the whole creation. All life forms from the lower to the higher have one and only intention, to raise their vibration and reunite with the source. This is a very long journey, but it is a motion that keeps every life form alive.

Wisdom of Thoth: The new human being

Do not try to explain artificiality. Do not indulge in analyzing and debating, shaping distortion into the polarity of right or wrong. Put all your effort into bringing yourself into a space of peace. A space of peace is about moving away from artificiality and distortion and entering the greatness of your being.

Absorb your greatness fully; make it your only truth and allow it to help you fulfil your purpose. Peace is an open door. All the gifts of the cosmos and Earth are using this door to enter your being and support you in this present moment. This flow of support is constant when you are in a state of peace.

Your body becomes an extension of Earth's body and then you know that you are created to live close to Earth and support her growth. Your everyday reality can not be an obstacle for you to experience Earth's intention. A distorted lifestyle has to be aborted and you should fully join Earth in order to transform and experience the Birth of a new human species. The ones who are willing to take this path are going to be the guides for others who are coming out of their hypnotic state and looking for direction. The new human being is an Earth being.

Introduction

People will need to create communities that allow them to experience growth. All united, will connect to their purpose and develop new skills for transmitting and receiving energy. Earth supports healthy communities that are able to grow following natural laws. She wants to be involved in our communities, she wants to offer her light but she also wants us to generate light and feed the whole planet. These are the natural laws and Earth was created to fulfil her purpose of a god-creator-planet, supporting the light of her beings.

Creating communities of truth and growth is the ultimate goal. The more human beings are able to connect to the truth in them the more clarity they will receive about their path, their unity with Earth and the creation of communities that will heal the schisms and bring growth. There were and there are still, a number of individuals who want to build communities in order to gain power over their members. An ideology cannot support those groups to create communities of light because what they are creating is a repetition of what already exists, the pyramid structure. If you are one of those people who want to join a community, you should go beyond mind manipulation and try to detect a pyramid structure, being the leading force and purpose. If you want to build a community, you should first connect to people energetically and then try to understand and develop their skills, abilities and purpose. Connect to their light and communicate their truth. Experience their greatness and open your doors so you can meet and create.

Wisdom of Thoth: Everything that is true carries light and supports growth

The cosmic being that you are wants to express its truth and create with the truth. It is time for humanity to experience collective growth and escape the long and tyrannical state of distortion and illusion constantly creating diversions, obstacles and illusionary rewards.

Humanity is called to purify from the multi-layered patterns, illusions, fears, confusion, self-destruction, anxiety and manipulation that are the fruit that hung from the tree of distortion and are feeding humanity and its creation.

Humans should create communities that focus on deep purification processes that restore the truth carried by Earth and all living beings that exist on the planet experiencing the same life flow and growth opportunities.

Communities should grow in all parts of the planet where humans purify with the support of Earth and her creation and tune into the collective growth. There is so much beauty, light and greatness in the life of a being.

Everything that is true carries light and supports growth not only in a human but in the whole planet. Your growth supports the growth of Earth and her creation and their growth is the abundance that creates all opportunities for collective growth to be created.

Communities of truth are going to be built and all Earth's creation united will receive and transmit pure light to the planet and allow the powerful state of the golden era to be created again and will be experienced by all beings on the planet.

Introduction

It seems that people find it hard to communicate, connect and love each other. Unhappiness and instability in a relationship bring disappointment. And very few things create disappointment as quickly as unmet expectations, the absence of true communication. How can we heal relationships and experience our most precious gift: to be powerful receivers and transmitters?

Wisdom of Thoth: Healthy relationships

Humans have many worries and anxiety about having relationships with other people. For many people, there is no truth or real joy in relationships. Everything is changing very quickly: people's emotions, expectations, behaviour patterns, and their ability to receive and transmit.

All these constant changes affect the path and purpose of the union between people. If you start to observe your relationship with others you will see that from the very beginning you were in a fantasy world. You are entering a relationship having no clarity about your true intention, you have no clarity about the other person's true intention and fantasy can create what is missing.

When human beings follow fantasies they are going to experience emotional roller coasters, excitement and great disappointment all at once. In the beginning, fantasies will create the perfect relationship in somebody's mind, people are looking at their partners and see the perfection they fantasize about.

When the fantasy and its illusionary expectations start to fade, behaviour patterns, fear and limitations come to the surface and create a different landscape. This can shock human beings and their reaction is to go into survival mode and the ego. This creates more layers of confusion and separation between people.

Some of you may ask how can I experience a loving relationship with others and whether is this possible on Earth. Your starting point is to love yourself and know who you are. People who do not love or know themself they create relationships that are based on need.

They need to be loved by others, they need their attention, their confirmation that they are lovable and often they demand this type of behaviour from their partner. Another behaviour pattern makes people give in order to be liked, and do things for others in order to get their approval. This can also lead to a loveless and complicated relationship. Human beings can not create relationships with others if they do not have a relationship with themselves. This connection can only be based on truth, a deep understanding of your greatness, your unique qualities, your path and your purpose in this lifetime.

Introduction

People on Earth exist in a false reality that takes away the power to connect to their true self and fulfil their purpose. When people start to wake up and understand the illusionary aspects of their thinking, experiencing and receiving, they find themselves on a mission to uncover the elements of illusion.

Only when you connect to your whole being, your true self, the Earth and the cosmos, you are able to receive healing and nourishment. In this state, you can accept everything you are and you will start shifting imbalances and blockages by going true a transformation. Purification is a process of transformation that can bring growth and support connections with your true self, Earth and the cosmos.

Wisdom of Thoth: Support purification on Earth

Human beings on Earth follow patterns that are created by distorted energies that bring thoughts, beliefs, polarities, fears, limitations and illusionary realities. There are also patterns that affect humanity as a whole and they are created by manipulation systems and controls that are using distortion and illusion to hypnotize and control human potential and growth.

This is why humanity exists in a multi-layered web of confusion, vulnerability and total separation from their true path and purpose. The hypnotic state that humans experience is a survival mechanism to help them deal with their artificial lifestyle and their lack of fulfillment and joy. In their hypnotic state, they are attracted to spiritual information and practices.

There are people who are totally unaware of their true path and purpose, existing in a hypnotic state that wants to teach others spiritual truths. These people will create entertainment that offers short-lived satisfaction and allows people to remain in their hypnotic state, follow their patterns and feed on illusionary beliefs.

The motivation of these teachers and students is not inner calling because they are not able to connect to their truth. These spiritual practices can create more layers of illusion and distortion that will spread to humanity and Earth. Human beings are polluting themselves with distortion instead of purifying themselves and connecting to the truth in their being. They need to know that their life purpose is to support purification in their being and the whole planet.

Introduction

Do not rely on your everyday patterns to create an existence for yourself and others. Your comfort zone should be constant movement, connecting to the Earth and the cosmos. Do not hesitate to listen to your intuition and make changes; these changes are the flow that guides you to your path.

People who have connected to the cosmic light and received healing and knowing they have experienced a deep understanding of their current situation and the way the divine plan is unfolding. When you exist in unity with all that you are and the cosmos then balance and growth will affect your being. In this state, you will be open to connecting to the source, receive guidance and nourishment from Earth, share and receive healing with humanity. This will make a physical being experience fulfilment and cosmic happiness. The path is open to you and there are no restrictions or rules to block your way. Growth can be yours if you choose it.

Wisdom of Thoth: Experience a new cycle of growth

Human beings on Earth may have experienced many challenges in the last two years and a common pattern may be the fear of losing people that you love, career prospects, and businesses that are failing. Some of you may experience great imbalances that have caused bad health, anxiety, uncertainty and confusion regarding your life path.

You may have worked hard to create something that was successful and brought you lots of joy but for a while, it seems to deteriorate or fade away. You may think that everything is collapsing and there is no support for growth or you may experience life in a survival state, trying desperately to cope with the challenges of everyday life.

I want to remind you that a living being goes through countless transformations; life is not a series of repetitive patterns where people follow a mechanical and repetitive lifestyle. Learn to see all challenges as an opportunity for growth.

Do not rely on your everyday patterns to create an existence for yourself and others. Your comfort zone should be constant movement, connecting to the Earth and the cosmos. Do not hesitate to listen to your intuition and make changes; these changes are the flow that guides you to your path.

Connect to your being, experience the transformations that are happening right now and be prepared to take steps and open up to opportunities that will initiate the next cycle of transformation. Often human beings experience problems in their lives when the mind wants them to follow something that has ended and the being is ready to receive the light, transform and experience a new cycle of growth.

Introduction

Accepting your multidimensional self is a step towards growth. Now we want you to live as a multi-dimensional being and experience life on Earth connecting your physicality with your astral growth. When you take this route you will feel the detachment from all artificiality and you will gain strength and knowledge beyond boundaries. Your connection with your astral body will start to be established and clarity will take over confusion and limitation.

All beings are working towards their unity with the source, the life-giver. There are many lessons and cycles of growth and evolution we need to go through in order to get to the higher planes. This is a natural process. I will say to you that our source created the Pleroma and the higher planes; the creation was closely connected to the source.

Wisdom of Thoth: Powerful creative forces

When human beings are able to experience unity within their being and then see themselves expanding towards the undivided and constant cosmic flow, they will not doubt that everything is created by the source and that they are also part of the source.

An analogy to help humans understand this is that their path was already created before they entered Earth. Earth beings are able to experience this path, see the wonderful opportunities that are stored there, create, heal and grow.

There is an interaction and there are processes of expansion and transformation when beings are connecting to their path or divine plan but there is also the truth that the flow of light in them will always exist and move towards the source even if human beings are fully unaware of it.

Living beings on the physical plane have the possibility of not being aware of their path and this is a unique form of learning. In the astral plane, living beings do not have this choice; they are constantly fully aware of their divine plan, the cosmic flow, the powerful creative forces and the intention of the source that holds everything together. The divine light is a powerful creative force in the cosmos because it experiences its being and divine plan within the beingness of the source.

Introduction

People on Earth are surrounded by clouds of distortion and often this is the state they experience everyday. Some of them are not aware of this and others are looking for remedies, healing, relaxation or enjoyment to help them disconnect from it.

Reincarnation is often a challenging experience for astral beings and this is why they need to prepare themselves and be open to their connections with their guides. When they are finally on Earth, they still have access to astral knowledge, but because of the low vibration on the planet, their connection with the astral plane can only be achieved in certain states like the dream state.

Your spirit guides support your growth and their intention is to help you escape the maze of distortion and illusion. They can see your purpose and want to pass this knowing to you.

Accepting your guides, you reopen the connection with them and you are able to receive guidance. When you are able to clear distortion and illusion, your connection with your guides becomes stronger. When you are able to be in a state of peace and not be affected by negativity, anger and disappointment then you will connect to your guides' support and guidance.

They are observing you and they want to help you find your way to your true self and purpose. They want to help you avoid diversions and open up to the cosmic light that will heal your imbalances and bring you clarity. When you are on your path, you will be able to connect to them and receive direct guidance. This is a connection worth maintaining.

Wisdom of Thoth: How to connect to your spirit guides?

All living beings are constantly supported by powerful creative forces in order to grow and transform because their growth supports life in the cosmos. You are constantly supporting and being supported by a vast energy field that allows the life flow to grow in all living beings.

If you are able to release all your limitations, that paint life on Earth as a path full of obstacles and struggles and you start experiencing the unity of the cosmos, then you will be open to all guidance that is coming to you through your guides.

The mind that creates limitations, the body that experiences these limitations and the restrictions that can affect your energy field can not support your connection with your guides.

All living beings have to purify from impurities that make them needy, desperate, disappointed, angry with others, and experience the fear of survival and a confused state of distraction. Some of you may say I need the guidance of my guides now to help me clear all my imbalances.

If you take a small step to observe yourself then clarity from within will come to the surface and help you recognize what is true and what is illusionary in your life. A small step toward growth can support you to follow the truth. Your intention and the steps that you take will open the doors to help you connect to your guides.

Your guides always surround you and want to offer their support. In a space of truth, you are going to create codes and forms of communication to help you receive guidance in its purest form. Your communication with your guides is only one drop of what is available to you and you are called to use your whole being as a magnet and attract the abundance of support that is available to you at all times.

Introduction

The Gods can maintain and create life when cosmic light goes through them. This is how they connect to the Source and become a creation tool. When the cosmic light travels to the astral plane, it helps beings to continue growing and transforming constantly and without interruption.

When the Gods receive cosmic light, they direct it to the astral plane because not only it is the largest plane but also an energy space of high growth. It is the birthplace of all beings. When cosmic light reaches the astral plane will continue its journey to all the other planes. All cosmic creation is united, receiving the cosmic light.

Existing in a peaceful state means that you exist in unity with your whole being and you allow the cosmic light to go through you connecting the astral and the physical body. When you are in a meditative state and you are able to disconnect from all illusion, negativity and artificiality, you exist in a space that is limitless.

You can experience constant growth like a flow of immense power of transformation spreading to your whole being. If you are able to remain in this state you will connect to the astral plane. You are opening up to unlimited opportunities for cosmic growth and this truth is transferred to your physical body.

Wisdom of Thoth: Human beings are powerful when they connect to their truth

Human beings will never stop asking questions, trying to clear the fog that they are experiencing right now. They are looking for the light that unites the Earth's existence and the cosmic greatness created by the divine and the cosmic light in the astral plane. All beings seek this powerful unity where their whole being as one is united to the Earth's high potential core and the astral plane and let the light create all exchanges and opportunities for transformation and growth.

The natural flow and path that gives life to all beings have the same route and they all meet and walk together on the same path: the flower, the tree, the river, the animals, the stones, and the soil are all experiencing the same flow of growth and transformation in order to reach the highlight of the cosmos.

Human beings are not created to be locked in an illusionary reality and ignore the powerful gifts that make their existence unique and everlasting. Humans are free and powerful to join all living beings who follow truth and create truth with them. In this path of collective growth, there are no winners or losers, bad or good, strong or weak.

The fear patterns, the survival instincts, and all negativity and limitations that can be experienced as a purpose will not support human beings to unite their whole being with the collective growth and the light. Do not ask your mind to give you answers that you can only get when you experience unity within your being, leading to greater unity. The cosmic creation in the astral plane will always exist because there is no separation; All beings are bonded with the truth of creation shared by the divine light.

Introduction

Your purpose is a life of truth, higher consciousness and your gift to support others to rediscover their true self. If you wish to be a creator, that is the path you have to take.

If all human beings on Earth could focus on creating a state of peace that is constant, the distortion would not exist; the lives of all individuals as well as the structure of their communities, will bring light to all. Maintain a state of constant peace for yourself and pass the experience to others. This is how we can truly help each other grow.

Your society and organizations of control will not help you to find your true path. If there was truth in your society, the illusion will not have a strong hold on you. You are responsible for your own growth and if you have a pure intention to connect to the truth then you will find the way to fulfil the divine plan of your reincarnation.

Wisdom of Thoth: Your true path is a flow of abundance

There are human beings who are able to recognize that their governments, organisations and social structures are restricting them, pushing them into a maze of fear and anxiety and the exit is nowhere to be found.

There are people who are worried about restrictions imposed on them. They worry about their ability to maintain peace and connect to their truth. They worry about what is coming and what additional restrictions will affect their lives.

In their state of fear, they will not stop pointing the finger not only at the people who bring these restrictions but also at the ones who follow them. In a state of fear, they can not see themselves. They can not see that they are constantly triggered, moving deeper into the maze of anxiety, experiencing vulnerability and separation that blocks them from being in peace.

You may hear them say: how can I be at peace when restrictions take freedoms away? I will advise these people to slow down, stop thinking and stop fighting. Return to your being, into your state of peace and connect to your true path. Your true path is a flow of abundance, truth and freedom. When you are fighting you are in the mind and the mazes of fear and anxiety. When you are in peace you are following your path and you share your light, supporting life on Earth.

Introduction

Our High Source has no form, personality or characteristics. Our High Creator is the perfection in the cosmos where everything is effortless, whole and limitless. High Gods can only dream to be in this state of absolute perfection, where there is nothing to see and yet everything exists simultaneously. Let's connect to this high perfection and expand ourselves to a limitless, eternal state by connecting to our creation code and the whole cosmic creation.

If you are aware of your whole being including your astral body, your higher self and your creation code then you can experience life in different realms and you can bring high wisdom to your third-dimensional reality. The purpose of all human beings is to connect to the cosmos, experience high growth and transmit cosmic light to Earth and her creation. The different realms are not in a certain numerical order; they cannot be defined and distinguished by your mind/logic. You should not follow the limitation of the mind but allow yourself to experience growth and unity with the cosmos.

Wisdom of Thoth: The mystery of Birth

All beings in all planes consist of their creation code. This part of their being is the highest part energetically and is connected to the light of our source. The creation code consists of all expected growth and evolution that one may have. Everything that you are and going to become when you transform is recorded in your creation code including reincarnations.

Before you reincarnate you exist in the astral plane. At the right moment, according to your creation code, you are going to be chosen to reincarnate or to exist in a certain plane. The astral being becomes aware of reincarnation, its purpose, and a general life plan. Then it goes through preparation in order to join the body that is created in the womb.

The unity between the female and the male parts can not produce a child if the energy of the astral being is not able to enter the unity of the male seed and the female egg. The physical body grows like a plant coming out of a seed; this is a natural process and is related to Earth's way to create.

For Earth, the birth of a plant, an animal or a human being follows the same process of creation. The physical body that grows in the womb attracts the light of the astral being and tries to help the energy find its way and connect to the physical body that starts to form. This is the true mystery of birth and is a complex process depending on many different factors.

20

The parents are also involved in this divine unity and there is a great transformation taking place that affects everybody's growth. Often the energy of the astral being is supported by guides who are able to connect to the physical body and prepare the unity that is about to take place. If the astral being is not able to connect to the physical body then the foetus dies either before the birth or straight after. This is a brief explanation of the birth of a human being.

Introduction

There are many people on Earth who are looking forward to the new paradigm, dismantling the old structures that hold humanity and Earth back from growth. They are waiting for great changes to happen and fantasizing about a life of great freedom, truth, unconditional love, effortless healing, growth and support. It is believed that the new paradigm will wash away all illusions, distortion, limitations and fears and bring great truth, power, unconditional love, high healing and miraculous transformation and growth. This may bring a positive outlook to the way people experience their lives but can it truly transform them into the powerful, cosmic beings that they are?

Wisdom of Thoth: A new state of being

Some people believe that everything is collapsing; the old state of being for humans is forced to dissolve and a new path is created to support growth on the whole planet. Human beings should know that they have supported the old limited ways for a long time and many are still holding on to them. There are other people who cannot see the new state of being and they are not able to observe with clarity the old one either.

Most people on Earth are still wearing blindfolds and mechanically follow the everyday patterns that take them to the same limitations. For many, the truth is the illusion and artificiality that is offered to them by the different sources of distortion including manipulation systems that are created on Earth.

Everything mechanical that determines your understanding of yourself and your life is part of the old. All experiences that created limitations are part of the old. A state of being that restricts you from being peaceful, free, and blissful is part of the old. A life that does not allow you to connect to Earth, experience her abundance, unity, and effortless growth is a life that human beings have experienced for centuries.

All this is collapsing right now and you will be asked to enter a state of peace and open yourself to receive the new. Humanity is standing at a crossroads. They are placed in front of a true path but there are also diversions related to the old patterns and beliefs. Enter a space of peace, purify from the old distorted patterns and see that your path and Earth's path is one. Becoming one with Earth is the high growth that will bring a new state of being.

Introduction

Meditation is an effortless way to go deep into your being, connect to your light, communicate with your physical body and experience the powerful abilities of your energy that help it expand, receive and transmit light. In a meditation state, you become aware of your great gifts and your true path and this helps you to purify from limitations and imbalances and disconnect from the mind and distorted realities.

Wisdom of Thoth: The fundamental element of meditation

Human beings in the western world have discovered meditation, exploring old spiritual traditions. They have created many different types of meditation and each type is linked to a specific form of healing, transformation, or it appears to be a vehicle to guide them to their true path and unique abilities.

This plethora of meditation techniques reflect the countless illusionary choices of modern times. Are these meditations leading to the true path of humanity to exist in harmony, peace in unity with Earth and her creation? The fundamental element of meditation is for people to experience peace and maintain this state.

Meditation has no time limit but it is a state that you want to grow and experience constantly. Meditation is not a break from your busy life but it is the foundation for building a life that reflects the perfection and greatness of who you are.

When people are asked to maintain a state of peace, all the imbalances and limitations will come to the surface and will interfere. If people are not able to be in a state of peace they have to observe their limitations. Never abandon this great gift, the gift of peace, because when you fully experience it is going to offer you another gift, the gift of truth. When you know your truth you cannot be entangled in illusion.

CHAPTER II

Connecting to your true self, you are connecting to your astral body and experiencing the growth that takes place in the astral body. You can exchange energy, receive high light and connect to the creation of our source. You can do all that when you turn your back to illusion.

Introduction

Some of you are seeking enlightenment but you are not moving forward on your path. Yes, you have to act, you have to make decisions, and you have to change your life. Everybody can grow because this is a natural law for all beings.

Human beings are always guided towards empowerment and their natural ability to fulfil their purpose on Earth. They are always supported to experience their true path connecting to opportunities and guidance but they prefer to close their eyes and detach themselves from their divine plan and cosmic existence. Human beings have the power to create their own life, reflecting the divine plan, receive light and help others receive the light too.

It is time now for humanity to understand that their astral growth and their purpose on Earth are connected and when they are able to understand and experience their purpose on Earth they will instantly receive astral growth. This is a great gift and gives humans the opportunity to exist in two different planes; they have this ability because they are perfect receivers and transmitters of light. All living beings on the planet are designed to be powerful receivers and transmitters of cosmic energy that need to wake up and fulfil their purpose.

Wisdom of Thoth: What is the astral plane

The astral plane is a space of constant growth and transformation and the home of all living beings. All beings that reincarnate on different planets and sub-planes, have experienced astral existence. The astral body is the permanent existence of a being and will never be interrupted or come to an end similar to reincarnation cycles. Physical and astral bodies exist in unity and are able to communicate and share light.

The process of reincarnation starts in the astral plane where a divine plan will be created and an astral being will be selected to experience a physical existence on a certain planet. Light will leave the astral and enter the physical body that is formed in the womb. All physical bodies carry the light of their astral existence and part of their purpose is to become aware of it.

Becoming aware of your astral existence will help you see clearly the purpose of this lifetime. You are a cosmic being that has immense power to create greatness and offer countless opportunities for growth to all life that coexists with you. When you connect to the light in you, one of your main gifts will be revealed to you: you are a receiver and transmitter of light; you bring the light of the cosmos to the physical body that you are and all physical bodies that connect to you.

Introduction

The following teaching shares information about reincarnation and how astral light moves into physical existence and offers empowerment and guidance for the continuation of all growth processes. Human beings will empower themselves when they connect to their light and allow astral existence to guide their physical experience.

The imbalances in our physical body are caused by the lack of communication between the physical and the astral body. This communication can be done by allowing your bodies to connect and regulate the light and energy that flows through them. The dialogue between all planes should be clear, constant and truthful. Different planes converse through the creation code which unites all. Communication is energy that flows through to assist with balancing, strengthening and creating. Listening to the communication between your bodies is a very special skill practised by masters on Earth.

Wisdom of Thoth: Are you aware of your astral existence?

Human beings are not aware of their astral existence. They are not aware that in their being they carry light that is responsible for initiating all processes of expansion and regeneration in them. The light that they carry is this part of their astral body that agreed to experience this reincarnation and is fully aware of the divine plan related to their current lifetime on Earth.

The light that moves from the astral body to the physical existence in order to create a new reincarnation, supports Earth to create a physical body. This new body will have the ability to receive and transmit light and stay united with the cosmos. The creation of a being is a gift that Earth can receive when she is open to receiving the high light and co-create with the astral plane. All reincarnations are Earth's opportunities to connect to the high light of the cosmos and co-create with it, allowing receivers and transmitters of light to experience life as Earth beings.

The creation that takes place on the planet, always involves an astral being bringing light to Earth. This connection enables her to create life, and support processes of collective growth and cosmic unity to be experienced by all living forms. All human beings are created with the ability to receive and transmit light and have an effortless path of constant transformation. Their astral light in them is guiding them to this path.

Introduction

Earth is open to receive the light that is coming from the astral plane because it supports her ability to grow and create. The light will travel from the astral plane and reach Earth's energy field, moving through all energy points, all layers of her physical body and finally will reach the core of her being. It will remain at the core energizing and transforming Earth's creative powers and all the opportunities for growth that lead her to the path of a creator.

Wisdom of Thoth: The cosmic light is entering Earth

When human beings reincarnate on Earth, the astral plane enters the Earth plane. The light of all astral beings that reincarnate on Earth is needed to build bridges for the cosmic light to enter Earth and support growth and transformation on the planet. When the light reaches the planet, it will spread from her energy field to the outer parts and finally will reach the core of her being. It will remain at the core energizing and regenerating Earth's creative powers and all the opportunities for growth that lead her to the path of a creator.

Earth's truth exists in the core of her being and expands to each layer of her body. One of the illusions that affect the human mind is that life exists only on the surface of the Earth. This illusionary belief is responsible for humanity's limitation to connecting to the planet's whole being and becoming co-creators. Humans are called to understand that the whole planet is a living being; the core of Earth has created the different layers and outer parts and the life flow is uniting all physical life and energy points on the planet. For human beings to become co-creators with Earth, they have to experience the power of the core that creates life on Earth. The ability of the core to create is related to the direct and uninterrupted connection with Earth's astral body.

Some of you may ask: what is the connection between a physical and an astral body? The light of the astral being will enter the physical body and exist in the core of the being. For growth to happen, all parts of the being are tuned to the core and receive high light and guidance in order to fulfill the divine plan and path of a living being.

Introduction

The following teaching offers great insights as to the essence of the source and its ability to create. All beings are created by the light of the source and this is how they communicate, stay connected and grow with the source. The cosmic light brings life to the whole cosmic creation. When you connect to it, you connect to everything that exists. You are in communication with the Source and this communication can transform you, heal you and support your rebirth.

Wisdom of Thoth: Connecting to the high light

The light in all beings is constantly expanding in order to move to higher planes and finally connect to the Source. This is how creation grows and regenerates itself. All beings have a natural ability to grow to higher planes and the energy fields and grids support this growth.

There is constant communication within your being, between you and your astral body, higher self, and creation code. This communication can be seen as an energy exchange that creates countless opportunities for growth, guiding you on your path. All beings want to connect to the source because it is important to renew the starting point of their creation. This can only happen when you connect to your creator through energetic communication.

Some of you may ask what is the Source? The source is the highest creator light and all cosmic life is created by the light of the source. In the same way that Earth is supporting her creation by allowing growth and nourishment to enter all living beings, the source creates a life that exists in unity with its light. There is no separation between all life that exists in different planes and the light of the source.

Some of you may want to ask what created the source? The beings that exist in the astral plane have no beginning or end; they have unlimited opportunities for transformation and empowerment; they can receive and transmit constantly. This constant movement of light that brings life to all beings is the intention of the source. The source is in constant movement, regeneration, and growth and this is why the qualities of its life are constantly being renewed and its existence and ability to create have no beginning or end. People can describe the source as self-created but there is another form of life that is supporting its creation.

Introduction

The physical body and the astral body are designed to be connected. All human beings can observe and communicate with their astral body when they are able to connect to the core of their being. The core is the most powerful part of a human because it carries the light of the astral body. The light in the core of your being is a powerful navigator and guide that knows your path and the opportunities created for you in order to experience an effortless life on Earth.

Wisdom of Thoth: Tuning to the core of your being

All humans are able to connect to the astral plane because it exists in them. It is the light of their astral existence that travelled to Earth and co-created with her their physical body and energy field. The body is grounded to Earth for nourishment and the energy field can receive powerful energies to support the growth of the being. All living beings including animals, plants and elements carry the light of their astral existence in them, and this is the bond they share.

Their core cannot be affected by any distortion or illusion and when all parts of their existence are tuned with a core, the being can experience a life of effortless growth. Growth processes such as purification, healing, transformation and expansion can be experienced on Earth when all life is able to connect to the core of its existence. Living beings on Earth can connect to the planet and her creation with the light in the core; this is how they receive and transmit light, support each other's growth and be part of Earth's divine plan.

The energy field of all living beings is part of Earth's energy field and this is how they can experience collective growth constantly. The astral light in the core of your being is teaching you and Earth, cosmic laws and cosmic unity. It creates opportunities for all living beings to experience their true, effortless and uninterrupted path of growth and fulfilment. The light in the core of your being knows your path.

Introduction

The following teaching shares wisdom about the light within, the core of our being, cosmic seed and soul. The light that moves from the astral body, entering the Earthly existence carries the divine plan that will affect the life cycle of the light being of the reincarnated. When the light leaves the astral body it is supported by a connector, the soul. The soul is a non-physical entity that is an integral part of the light of the astral body. The soul has a very special purpose: to be the vehicle for the light to enter physical reality. The soul remains attached to the being for the whole reincarnation and at the end of the physical existence, it will become the vehicle that will bring the astral light to the astral body. The soul supports the connection between the physical and astral body.

Wisdom of Thoth: The cosmic seed is in you

The light in your being supports the growth and transformation of the cosmic seed in you. In the first phase of reincarnation, a powerful transformation is experienced by the astral being: the creation of the divine plan of the new cycle of growth will initiate the astral light entering the multidimensional space where the physical body is going to be created.

The astral light will enter this space first, creating the core of the being which is a cosmic seed; it is a portal to the being's divine plan, leading to a higher dimensional existence, the astral plane. When the light leaves the astral body, it is supported by a connector, the soul. The soul is also created by astral light but has a very special purpose: to be the vehicle for the light to enter physical reality. The soul remains attached to the being for the whole reincarnation and at the end of the life cycle, it will become the vehicle that will bring the light to the astral body. The soul supports the connection between the physical and astral body.

When human beings are able to experience their whole being, they can also experience the light in the core of their being. The power of their light cannot be described by terms and definitions that are born in the mind. When you connect to your light, you experience the cosmic force and powerful unity of the astral plane.

Introduction

Humans can free themselves from all limitations when they accept and experience this important truth that Earth's beings are not created to live a life of illusion, distortion, pain, fear, confusion or separation. They are created to exist in unity with the cosmic seed and to be guided by the light and have a life of continuous growth and transformation that is effortless and natural. This form of effortless existence is offered to all living beings to be experienced throughout their whole existence.

Wisdom of Thoth: The cosmic seed is a multidimensional space within

The astral light exists in a multidimensional space in you and this can be seen as the cosmic seed. Earth's energies can connect to the cosmic seed and create bridges between the astral light and the physical body and energy field. Astral light within the being supports everything that Earth has created in you and the way they all connect and experience the true wonder of this reincarnation.

A being on Earth is not created to live a life of limitation, pain, fear or illusion; it is created to exist in unity with the cosmic seed and to be guided by the light in order to experience a life of constant growth and transformation that is effortless and natural and can be experienced by the whole being. This is the path of all living beings on Earth.

When beings are able to see their path, they are connected to their light. Their path is filled with countless opportunities for expansion; to create with their unique gifts, connect to all living beings and support the collective growth on Earth. Their purpose is to become powerful receivers and transmitters of light that feeds, heals and strengthens their whole existence. They will be able to transmit their greatness to all living beings on the planet, creating a plethora of growth opportunities for Earth and her creation.

Introduction

We are all part of the unseen, formless, all-contained, all-created power of our High Creator and we are going to start our quest to high truth and knowledge from this point inside us which unites, generates and contains all that we are.

All life is touched by the divine light. We are all following the cosmic flow and we bring it into our being. The purpose of humanity is to become creators and experience their divine plan, the godly plan. We have the ability to connect to the cosmos constantly as the divine and the cosmic light reaches our being. When we are able to connect to Earth, we connect to the cosmos, follow cosmic laws, and create effortlessly then we experience the high light of the cosmos transforming our being.

Wisdom of Thoth: All life exists in divine unity

Human beings know gods through mythology and religion. For many humans, a god has a physical, masculine or feminine form as well as a light form and he or she is concerned about the lives of human beings. Mythologies share stories and human qualities and characteristics, depicting the colourful life of gods on Earth. When humans are not able to experience unity within their being, they cannot see that they are part of a living god and this is Earth and they are also part of a high creator and this is the Source.

The greatest illusion and suffering that humans have to endure is their illusionary belief that they exist separately from Earth and that if Gods exist, they are only concerned about the human civilization which is superior and therefore in separation from all creation. This belief makes humans receive and transmit illusion, focusing on the mind/ego limitation, and experiencing a life disconnected from their purpose and path.

33

When you connect to Earth and see how effortlessly she can create and nourish all living beings, you will know that she is a god creator following cosmic laws. Earth is connected to the cosmos, she is experiencing cosmic growth and she wants all her creation to exist in unity and create bridges for the cosmic light to enter her energy field.

The purpose of humanity is to become creators and be aware of their divine plan, the godly plan. When you are able to connect to Earth and the cosmos, follow cosmic laws, and create effortlessly then you experience the high light of the cosmos, transforming your being. Some of you may want to know about the gods of the Pleroma.

You may also want to ask: can humans be gods? The gods of the pleroma exist in high light and they are able to connect to the Source and create according to its intention. A simple way to explain the Source and its connection to the gods and the rest of the creation is the following: Imagine a human being that is fully naked, this human being would want to cover himself in order to feel safe, warm, and protected. He may also want to develop some tools to help him create. Then he is going to create his home, his garden, his neighbourhood, town, or country. The intention of this being is the light of the Source; the clothes and tools are the gods of the pleroma; his home and garden are the high planes where gods exist and everything else is the rest of the creation. The light of the Source is guiding the gods to create. This light is absolute unity and absolute freedom.

Introduction

Truth is one path and is not related to one's ideas or thoughts. Truth is the unique path that was given to you from birth. It is connected to a greater path, a collective goal of transformation and renewal. The divine plan is not concerned with survival. It supports the acceleration of growth and strengthens your ability to connect to your truth and receive the high light. Those who know the truth and have purity as their driving force, will be able to experience unity with the cosmos.

Human beings on Earth came to the planet in a pure state and should remain open to all the opportunities and support available to them to heal and disconnect from all products of distortion. Human beings will experience a moment of truth, a profound awakening, and they will receive this inner knowing that their thoughts and beliefs are not their true self.

Wisdom of Thoth: Moving away from distortion

All human beings have been given this opportunity in this lifetime: to break away from illusionary beliefs, fantasies, expectations, pain, and suffering and return to the greatness of their cosmic existence. Countless opportunities for growth are being created on Earth and are travelling toward the energy field of human beings.

A new layer of high light will surround their field and penetrate their physical body, reaching the core of their being. Humans will experience a moment of truth, a profound awakening, and they will receive this inner knowing that their thoughts and beliefs are not their true self.

They will also understand that when they ignore their true self, they allow the external forces of artificiality, illusion, and distortion to tie them into the limitations of an illusionary reality. They will be able to observe how illusionary realities can spread from one being to another and how people collectively nourish and give their power to their thoughts and beliefs to become their path.

If you wish to purify from fear patterns that hold you back, you have to observe your mind. You observe the intention of distorted energy coming from your environment and trying to enter the mind in the form of thought, feeling or sensation that are not part of your own pure intention which constantly guides you toward growth and transformation.

Moving from the illusionary reality to a state of peace, experiencing the greatness and the perfection of your being is a process of effortless transformation. Growth is an effortless and painless process in all planes, reflecting the constant flow of cosmic growth in the astral plane.

Introduction

The cosmic connection can provide all wisdom and all truths about all structures supporting life in all planes. Humans will have to experience this truth if they wish to have an effortless life on Earth.

Humans have free will and can be exposed to many different paths and life choices. They become trapped in distorted patterns and allow them to form into "truth" or "path" and guide them to follow diversions where they will remain trapped in a multi-layered maze of confusion.

The longer humanity remains in these multi-layered mazes of confusion the more disconnected they become from their true path and true self. So now humanity is called to observe the mind and the space that allows distortion to grow.

Distortion guides people to follow the survival fear state and the ego and move to more restricted zones of growth where they feel totally hopeless and lost. When this happens, truth, abundance, growth and the effortless path, all being cosmic gifts, become distant and unknown.

Wisdom of Thoth: Seeking truth

The astral plane is in your being; you can experience the cosmos in your being during your lifetime on Earth. When humans seek truth and cosmic wisdom, they focus on the mind and they get entangled in theories, beliefs, and ideas.

The mind creates a plethora of "truths" which are vulnerable and fragile and they can only survive if they reinvent themselves. Many layers of illusion and distortion will support ideas and beliefs to transform and reshape themselves in the mind. The people who accept and share these ideas will find themselves trapped in a multi-layered maze of confusion.

There are humans who are looking for truth in their being. They want to connect to the healing energies of their heart. They want to connect to the cosmos by transmitting energies of unconditional love and unity with all life. They accept that their heart is a portal that will guide them to cosmic truths known by beings in the astral plane who exist in high light.

Human beings will experience the heart center when they practise unconditional love and act with pure intention. It is time for human beings to expand beyond the limitations of the mind and explore life, travelling on unconditional love, purity, and unity.

When you are able to experience the cosmos with your heart centre, you will be led to another power within you: the light in the core of your being, the cosmic seed that is the true connection between your being and the astral plane.

Introduction

In the first phases of reincarnation, the astral light and Earth unite to create the physical being. The astral light confirms Earth's creative abilities to initiate the formation of a physical body and an energy field around it.

The core of the being is the multi-dimensional space that unites Earth and the cosmos. This connection is constant and offers continuous communication. Earth wants you to connect to the core of your being and experience the cosmic seed in you; the astral light and the wonderful gifts that are available to you, to support you reach the path of truth and purpose in this lifetime.

Wisdom of Thoth: What are the first phases of reincarnation

During the first phase of reincarnation, the astral light meets with the powerful light of Earth and opens her up to her ability to create life. The astral light confirms Earth's creative abilities to initiate the formation of a physical body and an energy field around it.

The core of the being is the multi-dimensional space that unites Earth and the cosmos; the residence of the astral light within the being. When Earth is called to create the physical body and energy field, she is aware of the being's divine plan. She wants to create a physical body that is fully tuned and connected to its divine plan.

The divine plan is carried by the astral light and exists in the core of the being. The core will go into processes of transformation and growth and create the truth of the being, its path, and purpose, and countless opportunities for growth and unity with all living beings.

Earth will create a body that can carry all these gifts and much more. She will teach the body to follow a unique movement, an effortless flow that unites not only the parts of a being but all of Earth's creations. She will teach the body to recognize and stay open to receive nourishment as well as to create nourishment for others.

Earth wants you to connect to the core of your being and experience the cosmic seed in you; the astral light and the wonderful gifts that are available to you, to support you reach the path of truth and purpose in this lifetime.

Introduction

The astral light that moves into the physical plane at the beginning of reincarnation is aware of the divine plan of a being and will share it with Earth in order to create a map of creation that will eventually transform into the true path of a being. The light will support this powerful creation within the being and will also create truth, greatness and all growth processes that link to an effortless path related to a being's reincarnation.

When you follow your true path, you experience the multi-dimensional vastness of your existence. A state that is pointing at your power and greatness and it is in constant expansion. In this state, you will be given the ability to unite and heal your whole being; to experience the cosmic aspect of your existence, connecting, communicating and co-creating with your physical body and energy; then you will know that there is no truth in limitation.

Wisdom of Thoth: Your true path is a vast multi-dimensional field

The light of your being has created your true path which is a reflection of the divine plan. The astral light within your being is aware of your divine plan and purpose on Earth and it was given a special duty to create a path that will allow you to experience a joyful and fulfilled life on Earth.

Your true path is a vast multi-dimensional field full of opportunities for growth! Countless opportunities for growth exist around you and their constant regeneration and rebirth create this movement that is called an effortless flow.

When human beings experience the effortless flow, they are connected to their light and they are guided to their path. The world of limitation, fear and distorted beliefs is falling apart; human beings are able to accept and experience unlimited opportunities for transformation and the powerful gifts that the light in them can create.

When humans "go with the flow" they untie themselves from the restrictions in the mind and enter the truth of the being. When you follow your true path, you experience the multi-dimensional vastness of your existence.

This is a state that is pointing at your power to expand endlessly. You are given the ability to unite and heal your whole being; to experience the cosmic aspect of your existence, connecting, communicating and co-creating with your physical body and energy; and then you will know that there is no truth in limitation.

Introduction

The astral light cannot be affected by distortion, it cannot experience schisms or separation from the growth cycles on Earth and the cosmos. The powerful light in the core of your being can only transform when it reconnects with the astral body; its important duty is to support growth and transformation in your being in an uninterrupted, constant and unchanging way.

Wisdom of Thoth: The astral light is a pure creative force

The astral light that exists in the core of your being cannot be affected by any patterns of limitation. The light in your being cannot be affected by illusionary and distorted beliefs or suffer from imbalances that affect the mind, body and energy.

It cannot experience schisms or separation from the growth cycles on Earth and the cosmos. The powerful light in the core of your being can only transform when it reconnects with the astral body; its important duty is to support growth and transformation in your being in an uninterrupted, constant and unchanging way.

Human beings are created to experience their light as a powerful force that can initiate transformations and growth cycles in their body and energy field. Connecting to their light, human beings experience this effortless flow that leads them to their path and purpose and all-natural and cosmic truths.

When human beings connect to the light within the core of their being, they are rewarded with powerful gifts to help them experience the truth about their purpose on Earth, their unity with all life, the gift of knowing, the gift of being a receiver and transmitter, the gift of creation and the gift of transformation and growth.

The light in the core of your being is not Earth's creation; the physical body and energy of a human being carry Earth's vibration and follow natural laws and the light creates bridges for the high growth in the astral plane to enter Earth's creation.

Introduction

The following teaching wants to stretch that connecting to the powerful light within you will have access to all cosmic truths and you will be able to fulfil your purpose on Earth. The light in you carries cosmic wisdom and teaches every part of you to grow and transform, to purify and heal, to expand and unite with all life. When your whole being experiences unity, all growth processes intensify and you can finally disconnect from the limitations of fear and illusion.

Wisdom of Thoth: The light will teach you cosmic truths

The Light in your being experiences cosmic unity. It has the ability to connect to all living beings in all planes and receives cosmic growth. The astral light is not restricted to existing in your physical body and energy field but is constantly reaching out to the astral body and its light.

The light in you is a powerful receiver and transmitter of cosmic information regarding astral growth and creation. The light passes cosmic information to your being in order to teach all parts of your existence to experience expansion and unity with all life.

The light will teach your energy field to grow and expand toward Earth and the cosmos. You will connect to the energies of other living beings, communicating with their light and receiving support and healing. Your energy can connect to the powerful energies in the core of the Earth and experience her pure intention, purpose, creative abilities and growth processes.

Expansion and growth can also be experienced by your physical body. Its motion; its ability to heal and restore itself; its rebirth and re-generation; the communication between all parts of your being; its connection to your energy field and all processes of empowerment and transformation. All these are happening to your being right now, in this present time.

These beautiful gifts that the Light shares with you are the power of life. In this reincarnation, you are called to carry the flame of life with your whole being and you will also learn that you cannot control life to create in you. The seed of all life was planted in the high planes by the intention of our Source and life on Earth is a leaf of this majestic tree that is free to grow for eternity.

Introduction

Limitations can be experienced by most human beings every day and affect everything they do. There are many reasons why this is happening: distortion exists in their environment and is being shared by the people they meet and socialize with. Distortion also shapes their own patterns, expectations and understanding of their life and purpose. When human beings start to observe their mind and demolish the towers of illusions created by distortion, they will reconnect to their light and the whole being. Make it your everyday focus to empty your mind and connect the whole being to the light in your core. This is when life becomes effortless.

Wisdom of Thoth: The light is connecting you to your path

When living beings are able to experience the light in the core of their being, they will be taught to disconnect from the illusionary and distorted diversions in the mind and instead follow their true path.

The light in the core of your being can initiate and support the process of growth and transformation that will lead you to your path. Your path is a multidimensional state and for you to enter you have to connect all parts of your being to the light that you are.

The light should nourish, guide and create strong bonds with all parts of your physical body, mind and energy field. Your light can penetrate every living part of you and unite them to cosmic perfection. Cosmic perfection is the ability of a being to experience unity with all creation and be in constant transformation.

Your light will show you the perfection of the cosmic laws and will encourage you to unite with Earth and her creation, becoming a powerful receiver and transmitter. When your light becomes the force for growth in your being, a powerful flow will be created that can guide you to your path where you can experience countless opportunities and develop extraordinary abilities.

Human beings are confused and in separation when they allow the mind to become the driving force. Illusionary realities, distorted beliefs, confusion, limitation and fear are what the mind absorbs from the environment and turns into reality. Life is not an effortless flow, there is no unity and perfection when the mind is entangled in patterns of distortion. Empty your mind and connect the whole being to the light in the core of your being. This is when life becomes effortless.

Introduction

The more we experience greatness the closer we come to the core of our being and the light in us. Some of us may be a little confused about greatness when the mind is constantly pointing at limitations, restrictions, challenges, blocks and imbalances. Greatness is a cosmic law linked to constant growth. Earth, being a powerful creator, is constantly creating growth and greatness in all living beings.

All beings experience growth and carry greatness. This is how they are going to know their truth, path, and unique abilities and see all these gifts in other living beings around them. It will become clear that all living beings have a path and a purpose, they are all receivers and transmitters of light and they are called to unite and co-create with Earth.

Wisdom of Thoth: Will you follow the ego or inner greatness?

The light in your being will always guide you to unite with the truth of your path and help you experience the effortless flow of growth and transformation. When you experience an effortless life you can also understand that everything around you carries light and is growing with you in an effortless way.

In a true and pure state, you connect to Earth: her powerful creative powers, her light, her truth and purpose as a living being and creator. Connecting to Earth is an awakening that takes you away from the limitations of the mind. If your intention is to live an effortless life on Earth, you naturally break away from the illusion and limitations in the mind and accept the greatness and perfection of your being.

The more you experience greatness in your everyday life the closer you come to the core of your being and the light in you. This is how you are going to know your truth, path, unique abilities and see all these gifts in other living beings around you. It will become clear that all beings have a path and a purpose, they are all receivers and transmitters of light and you are called to unite and co-create with Earth.

When you follow your ego you break down true communication with your own truth. The ego is a survival mechanism and when people focus on the mind every moment of their lives, the ego becomes the obstacle to true growth.

When you connect to other people in order to grow and create with them, you have to be in a pure state. In a pure state, your whole being experiences balance and is nourished by the high energies of the cosmos and Earth. When human beings feel the need to force each other or to go against their family and friends, they are following diversions that are dictated by the ego.

You can only connect to others when you are in a peaceful state, focusing on your growth and sharing your growth with others. This exchange will bring unity and the high light will enter the being of all people who are connecting and sharing light. Human beings have to observe the activity in their mind and the interference of the ego. Feel free to transform your life and enter a state of peace.

Introduction

Human beings are responsible for their current state because they have allowed it to grow in them and make strong roots. At their birth, they were given all the tools needed for this journey. They were born with healthy bodies and unpolluted minds. Physical body and energy were tuned into the core of their being and were fully aware of their purpose and path. They had a passion for life and they were able to share their light with others.

Patterns of limitation start to grow when human beings disconnect from the greatness in their being and start observing the illusionary world around them. Young children are forced to think of their future role in society. They are programmed to accept illusion as truth and completely ignore their purpose and the divine plan of their reincarnation.

Wisdom of Thoth: Leaving the mind

Preparing to leave the mind and enter the being should be an effortless experience because you become free from all limitations: instructions, methods and the fear of failure. For years, you were following a very detailed map that was not part of your being; it did not carry the growth opportunities of your multidimensional being or the power of your light that constantly grows and regenerates itself.

When you move away from the mind, you experience life without perceptions and beliefs that can create schisms and divisions. The freedom and effortless flow are not ideas and thoughts but the growth and transformation in your being.

An important step to purification is to empty all mind structures that want to build a reality for you. Release beliefs, thoughts and perceptions; you cannot rely on them to receive true understanding and clarity. Release patterns, fears, negativity and limitation; step into the limitless power that you are and learn to experience the vastness of the present time. Life becomes an expansion when you empty yourself from all mind structures and come into the known; the true self.

CHAPTER III

Only when you purify and go through a rebirth, you will be able to experience high growth. Connecting to the cosmic light and purifying yourself are gifts you can give to others and together you can co-create this space of truth and high light. Healing and unity are necessary for the growth of all living beings. When you act with pure intention you are able to connect to your whole being and the Earth and start growing in unity.

Introduction

The greatness of a being is so vast and powerful; it cannot be conceived or shaped in any form known to the human mind. It is a portal where all intentions of truth unite and build vast structures of cosmic creation. The greatness of a being may appear as a seed of growth when placed in a microcosm but it is truly a unity of all opportunities, all cosmic laws and all paths of transformation that are taking place in the cosmos in this present moment. Greatness cannot be fragmented or divided; it expands beyond all limitations and it will support you on your path.

Wisdom of Thoth: Truth is in you

Astral beings reincarnate on Earth, having to walk a path that reflects their divine plan; their opportunities of growth on the planet are linked to astral growth. They are aware that during their reincarnation on Earth, they will be given countless opportunities to empower themselves, transform and fulfill their purpose. They are also aware of their multi-dimensional existence, the unbreakable and everlasting connection with all cosmic creation and their astral light, entering their Earth body and guiding them on their path.

All connections of growth, transformation and expansion are mapped out in their divine plan and the astral light that exists in the Earth being, carries the truth that will be spread to every cell and energy point in your being. The light is guiding you to walk the path of truth, experience an effortless flow and support unity and collective growth.

The light will guide you to fulfil your purpose on Earth, to experience her body being your body and her energy being your energy. The light in your core will bring unity and growth to your whole existence, nourishing your multidimensional being with the truth of your divine plan.

The light will guide you to experience countless opportunities of expansion offered to your Earth being and the power of unity that supports cosmic creation. At the end of the life cycle, the light will guide you to experience a series of transformations that will prepare you for the intense purification process during the transition time. When you allow the light to guide you, you understand that the purification process is necessary in order to maintain a flow that unites life and death, Earth and the cosmos.

Introduction

People on Earth understand their existence, being the physical body and the mind. They see the body as a group of separate components that are not able to communicate or support each other. They see the body as a machine that is controlled by a device, the mind, which is supposed to be able to gather information and send instructions to all parts of your being-machine. You understand growth as a bumpy road that will take you through different challenges, hopefully leading you to the highest part of a social-pyramid structure.

You probably know people who try to convince you that they are superior to you. You may also observe social structures supporting pyramid structures, dividing individuals, labelling them, limiting them or making them go against each other. People who are accepting these illusions as their true life path, are far away from the flow of cosmic unity.

I am here to connect you to the light of the cosmos, to Earth and experience cosmic growth. Being your true self will lead you to an effortless life. Connecting to your astral body will help you receive the cosmic light and transmit it to Earth and her creation. When you exist in unity with the cosmos, it will help you disconnect from your imbalances, all illusion and fragmentation on Earth and help others do the same. We all have an important duty and this is to fulfil our purpose and growth. This should be your intention and your guide in this reincarnation.

Wisdom of Thoth: Multidimensional Beings on Earth

The birth of a physical body is not a limitation in the cosmos; it does not block the astral light within the being growing and communicating with the astral body. The physical body is an integrated layer of a much bigger structure; it supports the creation of a multidimensional being that has life experiences on Earth and can maintain its connection to astral existence. The multidimensional being is a seed that goes through countless transformations and is supported by powerful creative forces. These powerful creative forces not only support its growth but they make a home in this new being.

All creative forces that were involved in the creation of your being, exist in you and your whole existence is a portal that leads to these powerful life-creators. Life is continuity, flow, unity, collective growth and transformation. All these are gifts being received and transmitted to all creation by the creative forces of the cosmos. The end of a life cycle that most human beings understand as the death of the physical body is part of the life flow; a process of multiple transformations that lead to transition and purification.

All creative forces that supported the birth are going to be present, designing the transition time. One of these forces is the light of your astral body, being supported by the light of the cosmos and all empowering Earth's creative forces. The light within your being will be the one that will disconnect from the physical body and energy and allow them to reconnect to Earth and become a layer of her body.

This is only one phase of the transition and purification and should be experienced as a flow. All transformations and growth processes should be experienced as a flow that brings more expansion and creates more opportunities for new transformations. A human being should experience joy moving from one cycle of growth to another; even if the life flow takes humans to the end of a life cycle, joy should not end. This transition will be another wonderful transformation, leading to another powerful unity and expansion.

Introduction

On Earth we experience duality which is a separation of self from all that exists. There is always a fight between opposites which is the cause of fragmentation and illusion. If you wish to evolve beyond polarity and fragmentation you have to disconnect from the idea of opposites. In nature there is no fight against two elements, there is only a union of the elements, bringing new life. People on Earth understand the world around them as a polarity of good and evil. This is a characteristic of the third-dimensional perception.

Wisdom of Thoth: The transition between life and death

Human beings that allow illusion and distortion to create a life for them and then get lost in the maze of self-destruction, cannot experience an effortless flow of growth that has the ability to guide them through countless interconnected transformations and growth cycles.

All forms of separation, when they are not observed and healed, are going to move and expand through the being; they will affect the mind, the body and the energy field, as well as the balance, communication and unity that supports the living being.

When humans experience the schism of separation, they have no clarity. Separation in their body cannot guide them to their path and purpose and support them through the powerful transition, leaving the Earth plane and reconnecting with the astral existence in the astral plane. In a state of illusion, a human experiences separation that affects all aspects of their existence.

When you start observing human beings who have accepted distortion as their true state, you see the countless cracks and schisms that allow many imbalances to grow strong roots in them. The transition between life and death is another painful schism that brings enormous fear, anxiety, and confusion about what is coming.

Humans have to observe and disconnect from everything that tries to keep them divided, fragmented, or separated. In this present moment, you are observing all forms of separation turning into a veil that has been thrown over you, locking you into a distorted reality.

You have the ability to remove it by focusing on the unity of who you are. Your being is a unity, serving a greater unity, the cosmos. All growth processes that are created to offer constant re-birth to cosmic life, enter your being and create this effortless flow and constant growth leading to a continuous and everlasting rebirth. The end of a life cycle is a powerful transformation that can be experienced as an effortless rebirth bringing you back to the home of all creation.

Introduction

All astral beings who reincarnate on Earth are going through the transition of birth and death. To be free from the survival fear of the transition, living beings have to experience all life, all growth, and all transformation as one path. Birth and death are not polarities, do not go against each other; if they do, birth and death are seen to support a long chain of limitations that blocks the truth in your being. The way you live your life can affect the transitions that support your reincarnation. Resisting the unity in your being that is part of a cosmic flow, will affect all processes of growth and transformation including transition. The light will support the flow and this is how a being is supported on its path.

Wisdom of Thoth: Transition

There is a preparation that human beings can experience, leading to the final transition and the end of a life cycle. This preparation can take different forms depending on the person's ability to connect to their whole being, true processes of growth and all creative forces that support growth and transformation in this present moment.

When human beings are aware of their true life purpose and are able to experience life as an effortless flow, the preparation is just a natural flow taking them to the next cycle of growth. You are listening to your body and the communication between your energy field and the creative sources who have been celebrating your life on Earth by supporting growth and transformation.

You are listening to Earth's guidance that supports you to fulfil your purpose in this lifetime and this naturally leads to the end of a life cycle. Earth will be responsible for keeping the physical body while the light of a being will be released in order to follow its own journey of purification and fully reunite with the energies of the astral body.

The process of purification for a human being can start quite early when people are lost in illusion and distortion. It can appear as a series of wake-up calls or opportunities for human beings to inspire them to make changes in their lives, clear distractions and help them to focus on their body, maintaining a state of peace. The signs and calling leading to preparation will continue to present themselves and will teach you the importance of living a life of natural growth and fulfilling your purpose. This is the key to a natural preparation that will take the form of a growth cycle and will lead to a rebirth of a being.

Introduction

All growth processes are initiated at the core of a being. The light of the astral body that enters the physical body will form a cosmic seed and will tune the whole being into immense and powerful cosmic growth.

The cosmic light brings life to the whole cosmic creation. When you connect to it, you connect to everything that exists. You are in communication with our Source and this communication can transform you, heal you and support your rebirth. The cosmic light enters your being and reaches all parts of your physical body as well as your aura and energies. It brings balance and unity to your whole being; it brings clarity, to help you connect to your true self, the Earth and the cosmos. Human beings are created to be Earth's receivers and transmitters of light. This way the cosmic light will enter Earth and offer her healing.

Wisdom of Thoth: Going Inwards

The preparation process that is necessary for an effortless transition and the end of a lifetime is going to take humans inwards and create opportunities for them to experience the core of their being. In the core exists the cosmic seed and the light of the astral body that has supported the creation of the multi-dimensional Earth being.

Human beings that follow their path, will have countless opportunities to experience the high light in them; they will allow its power to guide them through the countless transformations and growth processes and experience the fulfillment of their life purpose and the completion of their life cycle.

During the preparation process that was created to support an effortless transition and the end of a life cycle, human beings will experience intense detachment, a powerful release, moving away from the thought-jungle of the mind, focusing on the body and gradually moving away from the body too, all its sensations, pleasures, discomfort, memories, communication and focus on the light.

You will focus on the light in the core of your being because it is the only part of you that will carry life and continue its journey of transformation after the end of the life cycle. In this state, you will make peace with the past, you will accept and release it all. At the end of this process, you are becoming a diaphanous being, loving Earth and at the same time moving away from her. Earth is gifted with your essence and the lessons of your lifetime; your existence will create a tunnel for the cosmic light to enter the planet. At the end of a life cycle, the light that leaves the physical being will go through a powerful and intense purification process before it finally reunites with the astral body.

Introduction

The following teaching explores civilizations on other planets and the existence of the gods. Do gods communicate with other planetary physical beings? Can the divine light move through them and create growth and transformation? What types of civilizations can exist on other planets and do they need mythology or religion to understand and connect to the divine light?

Wisdom of Thoth: Civilizations on other planets

Some of you have wondered about civilizations on other planets. Are these civilizations supported by gods and in what way?

On Earth, mythology and the existence of gods have created many colorful stories. People of all regions, in all different eras, have created stories that made clear the existence of gods and their participation in Earth's growth. You have to remember that if human beings were able to connect to the high light of the cosmos and the powerful energies of the Earth, they were also inspired to create a new narrative, a new story to try to define their experiences.

Civilizations of humanoid beings exist on many planets and astral systems and naturally, they have created their own narrative regarding divine intervention. Similar to Earth, humanoid beings that had experiences connecting to powerful forces became the authors of this narrative and social mechanisms will shape it according to their consciousness.

Beings who carry a high vibration, do not rely on the narrative to define their connection with gods and cosmic creation. It happens through their being; they are open to receive and transmit light. Every single being has this ability and should not be restricted by social mechanisms.

The gods are carriers and transmitters of high light and the light that moves through them reaches every single being in the whole cosmic creation. The cosmic creation exists in unity; there are no separations or polarities. All beings carry life in them so they naturally have the ability to connect to the cosmic forces of creation and be supported by the highlight of the Source.

Introduction

The following teaching will offer you wisdom about the creation of the physical plane. The cosmic and divine light will move through the astral plane to create a foundation that will support the whole physical plane with its subplanes, star systems, planets and physical living beings.

For Earth, her physical body is her core and all other layers are the expansion of the core. This reflects the astral plane and the creation of the other subplanes: a natural expansion whose purpose was to bring more growth and unity. When the core of the Earth was created, the gods created a new divine plan and gave her new abilities to create so her physical form and growth could expand. She understood her purpose as a creator and saw this as a unique gift given to creators.

Looking at the core of the Earth, you will see that there were different elements created there to help the planet maintain life in its physical form. These elements cannot be found on the surface of the planet. Human beings have access to them when they connect to the core energetically and allow the high energies of the planet to enter their being.

Wisdom of Thoth: The creation of the physical plane

The first phase of growth that led to the creation of the physical plane can be seen as a unified flow that allowed planets and star systems to be created. The physical body of a planet was always attached to an astral body that was created on the astral plane. Physical bodies are not detached from their astral existence; they are an expansion of it.

The physical body was created by the cosmic and divine light carrying the intention of the source and moved through the astral body, creating a core for the new being that is not strictly physical. The core of all physical bodies is a portal that unites all life and its powerful creative forces in the being and beyond.

When the light creates, it will move through different portals and support the expansion of the core. When a physical body is created, the light will also support its ability to grow and transform. The light will create energy fields, energy points and connections. It will create powerful processes that the physical body recognizes as growth. It will also create other physical bodies that can support, receive and transmit light to all physical beings. The light will follow the cosmic laws and this is going to be the foundation and intention for all creation.

Introduction

Creation was experienced in many planets and allowed them to slowly build their own natural laws, focus on unique processes of growth in order to support their creation, and experience some independence from the growth in the astral plane, following new planetary laws. Each planet had its own laws and they supported creation processes, the growth of individual life forms, and ways to balance individual, collective purpose and divine plan.

Earth's physical body was created by the divine creative flow, which is powerful and effortless, guided by the cosmic light and the light of her astral body. The birth of many different life forms altered her creative intention and affected the balanced coexistence between all the beings that existed on Earth.

There was a moment in Earth's growth during the golden era when her whole physical body was touched by life, forming a mixture of microorganisms, plants, animals, elements, waters, mountain formations, and entrances to give access to all different layers to communicate and living beings to enter whole Earth's body. Earth's constant transformation supported her creative abilities but soon she was about to go on a diversion.

Wisdom of Thoth: The end of the golden era

When the planets and star systems grew and were allowed to expand creating their own living beings, they experienced a golden era, similar to Earth's golden era. For certain planets, the high dimensional state of the golden era was interrupted because the growth that they experienced was no anymore a unified flow. There was separation within the physical body of a planet and its connection with other physical bodies.

When destruction started to affect the physical plane, imbalances, schisms and the fear of survival started to grow in the physical bodies. This brought more separation and influenced beings to travel and colonize other planets.

This was an action that was not supported by cosmic laws and brought the end of the golden era.

When physical beings experienced a state of confusion and separation, they also started to seek cosmic and divine light desperately. They were disconnected from the grids, energy points, connectors and growth processes that supported the natural flow of light. This was the time that physical bodies will start to use external sources to help them reconnect. Beliefs, ideas, narratives, illusionary lifestyles and rituals started to grow but did not support the effortless flow of unity and the return of the golden era.

Introduction

In this teaching, we learn about the creation of the planet Mars. All planets in the galaxy have a unique existence and path and they were not created to co-exist. They did not carry the same light when they were created and the beings that exist on them were not part of the same growth and transformation process.

Mars was a planet that was created in the lower subplanes. The physical body of Mars did not grow to experience a golden era. However, the planet created resources that made it an attractive destination for astral travellers. Mars was not protected by energy fields that would restrict astral travellers from landing and exploring the landscapes. This gave them an opportunity to visit, create bases, explore ways to manipulate the planet's resources and elements as well as relocate.

Wisdom of Thoth: The beginning of life on planet Mars

The Earth belongs to a galaxy and co-creates with many planets in order to maintain life and her connection with the astral plane. All planets in the galaxy have a unique existence and path. They were not created to co-exist; they did not carry the same light when they were created; the beings that exist on them were not part of the same growth process.

Many of these planets were created on different subplanes and others were part of planets that were partly destroyed. There are planets that were colonized by many astral travellers who were not familiar with the planet's natural laws. These invasions caused great upheaval and confusion to the lives of living beings that were created on the planet; this often led to their extinction or living isolated in the inner parts of their planet.

Mars was a planet that was created in the lower subplanes. The physical body of Mars did not grow to experience a golden era. However, the planet created resources that made it an attractive destination for astral travellers.

Mars was not protected by energy fields that would restrict astral travellers from landing and exploring the landscapes. This gave them an opportunity to visit, create bases, explore ways to manipulate the planet's resources and elements as well as relocate.

Because of its easy access and its unprotected areas, many astral visitors were attracted and had to fight with others who tried to establish themselves there. Some of these astral travellers created civilizations on Mars. The wars destroyed parts of the planet and a plan for regeneration and rebirth made the planet split in two and the part that carries the core would enter a planetary group "similar to a galaxy" and start its renewal process, connecting to the light and supporting its growth and transformation.

CHAPTER IV

**The astral plane is a powerful receiver of the light of the
Source and when the astral plane transmits it, the light
becomes the powerful creative force that reaches every
energy point in the whole creation. When this happens the
light of the Source becomes the light of the cosmos.**

Introduction

This teaching wants to show that the whole life path can determine the type of transition that people can have at the end of their life cycle. If people experience a distorted life full of illusions and diversions, they should purify and enter a state of peace as a preparation for the end-of-life transition. When human beings come closer to the end of their life cycle, they withdraw from the people and the reality around them. They can no longer follow the stories of others and it seems that they do not have a story themselves to follow as they disconnect from the persona and the ego. Entering a state of peace will help people expand. Earth will support all.

Wisdom of Thoth: Prepare for transition

Human beings that experience life in their mind following distorted beliefs and aiming for illusionary rewards are given several opportunities for purification many years before the end of their life cycle. These opportunities are life-changing events whose purpose is to pull people away from the patterns of illusion and distortion and help them see their true path and growth potential.

These events are often seen as a crisis, collapse, major disasters, meltdown and can affect more than one person if there are more people who follow the same limited patterns. There are human beings who go through a process of awakening and start their own observation and purification process. They will observe their lives, beliefs that motivated them to take certain paths, their ambitions and expectations, and their fears and limitations.

You want to know who you really are, what is your purpose in this lifetime and how you can experience it. You are opening up to your true potential by observing and purifying from the old programming.

They will be people who will try to fix the crisis and go back to the same patterns without allowing an awakening to take place. These people are going to experience upheaval until the end of their life cycle. When humans reach the end of their life experience on Earth, they withdraw from the people and the reality around them. They can no longer follow the stories of others and it seems that they do not have a story themselves to follow as they disconnect from the persona and the ego.

Human beings that approach the end of a life cycle, are experiencing the transition already. The transition is a divine transformation; Earth will continue to support the path of this being; the light will enter the most powerful processes of growth that will enable it to return to the astral plane, the home of all life.

Introduction

Some of you may ask: why is it important to prepare for our final transition on Earth? All life is a series of transformations where all beings have to grow and experience re-birth; letting go of the old and moving into the new. The core of your being is calling you to connect to your physical body and observe its imbalances.

Ground yourself into a state of peace and focus on the communication with your physical body. Observe your energy travelling through your energy points, moving through all parts of your physical body. At the end of a life cycle, you are offered opportunities to connect to your Earth being, your path and your purpose on Earth. All living beings will have many opportunities to experience the greatness of their being and all the connections that support life. In all transformations, a human connects to the whole being and all the gifts of life.

Wisdom of Thoth: Final transformations

Human beings experience the end of a life cycle differently and this has to do with the preparation and transition that they were able to experience before their death. When human beings are not afraid or worried about reaching the end of a life cycle and do not desperately hold on to the realities and life patterns, they will experience what is coming in peace and share this with others.

All human beings, either supporting loved ones or going through the transition themselves, are learning from this experience and healing the mind from a major disease: the fear of survival. They will experience a release of thoughts, beliefs, polarities, separation, schisms and trauma. They will experience a flow that is more powerful that their mind-understanding and takes them to a space of acceptance, freedom, self-love and cosmic connection. There are also people who come to the end of their life cycle unexpectedly and for them disconnecting from the earthly sensations is a challenging experience.

At the end of a lifetime, people will stay connected to loved ones on Earth for a little while and soon after will enter a state of purification. The transition that human beings experience will lead them to a deep purification process that will allow them to observe their life, their divine plan, opportunities for growth, fulfilling their purpose, diversions, creation and sharing with others.

During this process, the human being that is now light, will extract the valuable lessons and let go of the rest. The final stages of purification will lead the light being to fully disconnect from the Earth reality, raise its vibration and start travelling through different subplanes until the light returns to the astral body and continues its astral growth.

Some of you may ask: what happens to the soul during the transition and purification process? The soul is a connector and supports the light entering the being that is about to have a life experience on Earth as well as leaving the Earth reality during the end of a life cycle. The soul exists in a space between the Earth life experience and the astral plane. It carries information about the divine plan of the current reincarnation and allows communication between the Earth being and the astral body. The soul becomes a vehicle for the light of a being to move through the different phases of purification and transition.

Introduction

At the end of a life cycle, beings are able to go through a deep purification process and experience all the opportunities for growth and non-growth that they had during their lifetime. During their purification, beings will understand their path and purpose and experience the divine plan of their reincarnation and how it is connected to their astral existence. Clarity and knowing about cosmic truths are coming back to their being.

Humans who were not able to purify during their lifetime, will carry the darkness of confusion even after death and will still remain in a confused state, standing at the crossroads without knowing where to go or what to do. Purification is a great gift given to the ones who are willing to experience growth, transformation and being supported by the cosmos.

Wisdom of Thoth: Moving to higher planes

The purification process that living beings experience at the end of their life cycle can be a lengthy transformational process and this depends on the attachments and blockages that human beings have experienced in their life and their ability or inability to purify themselves during their transition time.

When these attachments/imbalances/limitations cannot be fully observed and released, the purification process can take a long time and in some cases, the beings will not be able to return to the astral plane but they will be guided to reincarnate again. The light beings that are able to complete their purification process, will gently move through different subplanes and travel toward the high light of the astral plane.

Every time light beings enter a sub-plane, they go through major transformations that help them raise their vibration and acquire a new light body that will be able to carry high light. The journey through the different sub-planes can be long depending on the ability of the light being to flow through the transformation processes, release and regenerate itself.

During these powerful processes, the light being will keep releasing impurities and distorted energies and due to rebirth and regeneration will be able to open up and tune into the high energies of the cosmos. The astral body and the soul are supporting the light being to have a smooth transition and to reach the high phase of growth which is to be able to receive and transmit high energy. This will become the important work and the only purpose of the light being when it finally unites with the astral body and experiences the flow of its cosmic existence.

Introduction

At the end of a life cycle, a being goes through many powerful processes of purification and regeneration in order to travel to the astral plane and reconnect with the astral body. During these processes, the light that once experienced life in the Earth being, abandons its formal duty to guide and support the physical body and energy to experience its divine plan on Earth. The light is now free to fully untie itself from the physical plane and the natural laws of creation. Travelling through the various sub-planes, the light is going through a constant rebirth and every time is given a new purpose. When this purpose is fulfilled, the cycle of growth is completed and the light is ready to move on to the new sub-plane and go through a new rebirth.

Wisdom of Thoth: The journey of the light

At the end of a life cycle, the light of one's being, goes through an intense purification and multiple transformational processes, as it moves through the numerous sub-planes on the way to the astral plane. This is an intense growth practice that constantly accelerates, matching the growth of the astral body and its unique abilities to receive and transmit light, supporting cosmic creation.

During these processes, the light disconnects from its formal duty to guide and support the being to experience its divine plan on Earth. The light is going into a constant rebirth and every time is given a new purpose. When its purpose is fulfilled, the cycle of growth is completed and the light is ready to move on to the new sub-plane and go through a new rebirth.

When the light enters the energy field of the astral plane, the unity with the astral body will not happen instantly. The light will travel through the energy field, connecting to other astral beings and the growth processes that they are experiencing in the present moment.

This journey through the astral energy field will support the light to create strong bonds with life in the birthplace of all beings and experience the powerful astral magnets that support the constant movement of the cosmic light, reaching the whole cosmic creation. Some of these magnets will become responsible for the connection between the light and the astral body. This reunion will signal the completion of the task related to the light moving into a physical body and supporting the process of reincarnation on Earth. This achievement will carry certain gifts and one of them is to accelerate the growth of the astral body.

Introduction

There are so many powerful transformations taking place at the end of a life cycle and Earth will support human beings to experience this as an effortless flow. During the transition, every single part of a being will disconnect from this life experience and return to its creator or its place of growth. The physical body and energy will remain with Earth and the astral light with its vehicle, the soul, will move through many sub-planes and enter the astral plane.

Wisdom of Thoth: The new phase of growth for the astral body

When the light reaches the astral plane and re-unites with the astral body, the soul will also reconnect to the astral body. All light that left the Earth being, will find its way to the astral plane and the whole astral being, as one, will start a new cycle of growth. During the transition at the end of the Earth's life cycle, every single part of a being will disconnect from this life experience and return to its creator or its place of growth.

The physical body will remain with Earth and will exist in unity with her creation and creative forces. All astral light will return to the astral plane, the home of all life and reunite with the astral body. The new phase of growth for the astral body will be shaped by the new transformations and the truth that is carried by the light.

During the purification process, the light will be allowed to keep all the gifts that it acquired during the reincarnation on Earth: all transformations, valuable lessons, connections and exchanges with the planet, all guidance and creation will remain with the light and will shape the astral body's potential for growth.

The connection and energy exchange with Earth will also remain open and the astral body will become the energy point that will support and direct the cosmic light to enter Earth's field and physical body. These new connections are not going to be experienced only by the astral body but will affect the whole cosmic creation. These connections offer expansion and unity which are necessary for life to remain a powerful ocean without boundaries and limitations able to be in constant rebirth and unity with all.

CHAPTER V

All cosmic laws support growth and evolution. In the higher realms, life is not the physical body but it is often a unity of many energies that it is part of a complex electromagnetic field. An astral body cannot be seen or measured by your Earth understanding; it is a very complex unity of energies which is in constant movement and in connection with our Source.

Introduction

On Earth, human beings seem to forget their astral existence and this is because they are focusing on the body time-line and the physical reality that surrounds them. As the physical being grows it becomes affected by the polarities, the fear for survival and the traumas that affect Earth and her creation. If you wish to evolve beyond polarity and fragmentation you have to disconnect from the idea of opposites.

Astral beings exist in unity with the Source; they experience its light in their being in this present moment and this is what shapes their path. When human beings on Earth try to define their path, they fantasize about a chain of events, actions, achievements, failures, the people they meet, circumstances, locations, obstacles, beliefs, fears and limitations. These are temporary events that are not connected with the truth in the core of their being. Therefore their understanding of their path and purpose is illusionary.

Wisdom of Thoth: The perfection of an astral being

Astral bodies do not experience a static existence. They are in constant transformation; they are constantly receiving and transmitting the cosmic light whose intention is to move through the whole astral field and regenerate all life. Astral beings are never at the crossroads wondering what path to take because they do not experience confusion or schisms; they are a unified light in constant connection to the high light of the Source that is always nourishing their existence and supporting their life and growth experience.

Astral beings exist in unity with the Source; they receive its light in their being in this present moment and this is what shapes their path. When human beings on Earth try to define their path, they fantasize about a chain of events, actions, achievements, failures, the people they meet, circumstances, locations, obstacles, beliefs, fears and limitations.

An astral being exists in pure light and the thoughts, beliefs and stories of the mind cannot be attached to or penetrate the light. This is why at the end of reincarnation, the light of an Earth being goes through an intense purification and many more transformations and re-birth processes in order to unite with the astral body and experience life flowing in the light of the Source.

An astral body does not follow an effortless flow of existence, it is the flow. Astral beings will never experience any form of limitation, accepting as their birthplace the limitless and ever-expanding astral plane, its immense power to carry the light of the Source and its tremendous ability to hold and maintain life in the present moment.

The present moment for all astral beings carries the greatness and mastery of the Source; its ability to create life that will have the opportunity to transform and grow in order to support, maintain and balance life, becoming the flow.

Introduction

Many human beings want to purify and heal in order to enter a state of cosmic abundance. Their conditioning and limited understanding make them look around in despair for truth, using their mind and entering the dark channels of diversion and confusion. There is only one way to experience cosmic abundance and this is through your connection with the core of your being.

The inward journey will help you connect to the physical body and energy and you will finally reach the core of your being. The core is the cosmic point that receives the light and the intention of the Source; it is the first carrier, the first creation and the first creator. In the cosmos, all living beings are creation and creators and this is supported by all cosmic laws.

The energy structures in the astral plane were built as the core started to expand and went through countless transformations, regenerations and growth processes. The new fields supported the expansion of the astral core and the constant rebirth of the astral plane. Energy fields carry great light and this allows them to transform themselves and become an important element in the creation of an astral being.

Wisdom of Thoth: A creation and the creator

All of you who are connecting to these teachings at this present moment, are connecting to the core of your being and through this powerful point, you are travelling to the astral plane to experience cosmic growth.

Some of you may want to know about the astral body: what are the elements of its existence; what is the growth process of an astral being; how do they experience the light of the cosmos and the unity that supports life? The elements that created an astral body have also created the astral plane and through the countless growth cycles, all life went through multiple transformations supported by the light of the Source.

The intention of the Source and the light that overflows and is directed to create life are the most powerful elements of the astral plane. Another powerful element is the creation of countless micro-fields that are all connected and have access to the core of the astral plane.

The core is the cosmic point that receives the light and the intention of the Source; it is the first carrier, the first creation and the first creator. In the cosmos, all living beings are creation and creators and this is supported by all cosmic laws. The energy structures in the astral plane were built as the core started to expand and went through countless transformations, regenerations and growth processes.

They supported unity and communication as well as a balanced flow of life that was able to support all living beings. The new fields supported the expansion and the constant rebirth in the astral plane and they also had the opportunity to transform themselves and become an important element in the creation of an astral being.

Introduction

This teaching offers information about the creation of the astral plane by the light of the source. All living beings consist of a powerful core and their divine design is a microcosm of the macrocosm that is the astral plane. The core of the astral plane was the first organism created by the source. It went through many transformations and growth processes and finally became the place that will give birth to astral life.

Wisdom of Thoth: The core of the astral plane

The core of the astral plane is like a pool of light that nourishes all life as it perfectly reflects the intention of the source to create and maintain life in its creation. The core of the astral plane was created by the first drop of the intention of the source to expand and create a new life in its being.

Similar to a tree whose intention is to grow new branches, leaves and fruit and expand in order to remain powerful and true to its purpose as a powerful receiver and transmitter of light, the source is also guided to expand and grow.

The core of the astral plane was the first organism that was created by the source. It went through many transformations and growth processes and finally became the place that will give birth to astral life. The core of the astral plane carried the intention of the source for expansion but had its own purpose and growth processes. It became a vast living organism that can breed life so the light of the source can travel through energy fields and astral beings and support its expansion and creative intention.

The creation (astral plane) can become a creator guiding the cosmic light and the intention of the source. The cosmic creation becomes aware of the new life and its potential. As the astral core was created directly from the source, it inherited an immense power to create unique and highly vibrational life.

The core never carried low vibrational light; purification, healing and schisms never affected the core and all life that was created was perfect, a powerful carrier and transmitter of the light of the source. In the core of the astral plane were planted many seeds that became the foundation that supported the birth of astral beings and all organisms that support life.

Introduction

In this teaching, we learn that the cosmic light was created by the intention of the source and its purpose was to create within the being of the source. Cosmic light is a bond between the source and life. It is a form of communication between the intention of the source and the life that is forming and growing in the astral plane. Travelling through the whole astral plane and its subplanes, the cosmic light supports and unites all life with the cosmic laws and the intention of the source that offers nourishment, healing, guidance, expansion and supports every form of life to remain connected and in tune with collective growth.

Wisdom of Thoth: The cosmic light, a powerful navigator

What gave birth to the core of the astral plane was one drop of the source's intention into a space within the being of the source that was ready to receive and transmit, transform and create motions and elements that will take new life forms.

The cosmic light was also created by the drop of the source's intention and its purpose was to nourish and support the growth processes that will create life in the astral core.

Cosmic light is a bond between the source and life. It is a form of communication between the intention of the source and the life that is forming in the astral plane. But as the astral plane is expanding and transforming into a mega organism, the cosmic light is transforming too and it has its own high purpose. It is a powerful navigator, travelling through the whole astral plane and its subplanes, uniting all life with the intention of the source that offers nourishment, healing, guidance, expansion and supports every form of life to remain connected and in tune with collective growth.

The cosmic light will reach all cosmic seeds in all planes. It will strengthen the energy fields within their being and all fields that support cosmic unity and are constantly expanding toward the core of the astral plane. The cosmic light is received as a great gift, the all-knowing force of rebirth and transformation that has the ability to support all life forms and it is always present and ready to create. The cosmic light creates life within living beings and supports the flow of the source's intention to be experienced by the cosmic creation collectively and individually.

Introduction

Communication is energy that flows through to assist with balancing, strengthening and creating. Listening to the communication within your being is a very special skill that can support many growth processes. You will be able to communicate with your physical body and practice self-love and healing. Your energy field can communicate with the light of other beings and travel to the core of the Earth.

All these connections will bring lots of truth and wisdom into your being. You will be able to disconnect from mind clutter and instead experience your path and receive true guidance. When people focus on the sensations of the mind and try to communicate using limited language, they are missing the abundance that the life flow is creating. It is important that you are able to experience life as a whole being and allow the cosmic light to heal you, bring clarity and sustain inner communication and energy exchange.

Wisdom of Thoth: True communication

How can humans communicate effectively? What tools do they need to possess and what skills do they need to develop for effective communication? We are growing in you because we have the ability to communicate with you and connect to your energy. It is important that you know us and our teachings in your physical reality and to be able to connect to others through our teachings and light.

Language is an accepted form of communication and we want to use it in order to pass our light to the people of Earth. However, language can cause disharmony and confusion because it is a limited tool for communication. I want to connect to you energetically.

I want you to be able to absorb my light through these teachings and not try to capture the limited meaning of words. In order for you to connect to my light energetically, you have to develop your connection with your being and energy field. You have to accept me as the creator of Earth and the bringer of a new golden era.

You are energy beings and you have the ability to exist in different planes and experience different levels of growth. If you are able to develop your ability to communicate energetically then you will be able to connect to all parts of your being and experience life as a whole.

Do not rely on words to bring you the truth. Do not try to over-define words and their meanings in order to capture wisdom. Allow truth and wisdom to present themselves to you instead of you trying to paint a caricature of them.

The most effective communication is when people are able to be open to truth and experience it as a living being that can grow and expand at will. I am here with you to pass my light and help you to connect to your true self which is part of the cosmic truth.

I am the carrier and creator of the cosmic truth and I offer you a path of growth, commitment, and fulfillment. Open up to receive my gifts and you will soon be reunited with the cosmos and experience life as a whole being.

Introduction

If human beings on Earth did not experience distortion and fragmentation and were free to exist in a pure state, they would have an effortless connection with their astral body. Distortion, fragmentation and illusion are three main reasons that can cause astral paralysis.

This is why many human beings exist in a hypnotic state far away from their purpose, their powerful gifts and their true path. It is time now for humanity to understand that their astral growth and their purpose on Earth are connected and when they are able to understand and experience their purpose, they are instantly connected to their astral growth. This is a great gift and gives humans the opportunity to exist in two different planes being the perfect receivers and transmitters of light. Earth's creation includes many receivers and transmitters of cosmic energy that need to wake up and fulfil their purpose.

Wisdom of Thoth: Humanity's sleeping state

It was mentioned by many that humanity exists in a hypnotic state. The ears of humanity have heard this statement countless times and it seems that it does not have the power to wake them up. Instead of passively accepting that humanity is sleeping, perhaps it will be more useful if human beings described their sleeping state.

What is the effect of the sleeping state on your ability to see the truth and follow your path? How is your body reacting to this? What is your state of mind when you are struggling to wake up and you are still not able to fight the power of passive existence?

Perhaps you should observe yourself being in a hypnotic state and what is controlling you to forget and disconnect from the enormous potential of your being. Some of you may say that humanity does not follow collective growth; they separate themselves from it.

The sleeping state is the powerless state of a prisoner and there is a plan that humanity should be controlled and restricted in this state. There is only one way out. When you experience the power of the cosmos in your being you will untie yourself and you will support others to do the same. The sleeping state is an illusion and the creative power of the cosmos is the only truth.

Introduction

There are many people on Earth who seem to be satisfied, being in a sleeping state. They happily follow the social expectations and their thinking, actions and expressions are tailored to fit the same ideals. It is important to look the part of a successful member of society and this way you are accepted as successful. It is also important to mix with people who are also playing the part of a successful human. This way you think that your image is supported and stands out more. The people who follow this path become imitators of illusionary characters and their goals. In the end, you are fully disconnected from the purpose of this reincarnation and there is no way back to this knowledge which is cosmic knowledge.

Wisdom of Thoth: Escape the mind, experience your multidimensional being

The cosmic light in your being is constantly reminding you that you are a multidimensional cosmic being that exists in many planes and experiences many life forms. This is the prime law of your existence that will shape and reveal to you all opportunities for growth and transformation available to you in this lifetime.

Human beings who expect the mind to show them all truths, exist in confusion and ignorance. They see their patterns of limitation being their path, their struggles are their strength, their doubts are inner calling and their wisdom is their fight to escape survival and confusion.

73

Human beings who experience life in the mind are blocking all tunnels of communication with the light in the core. This limits their opportunities to experience life as a multi-dimensional being and explore the powerful gifts and abilities that can be stored in them.

The different forms of cosmic existence experienced by a multi-dimensional being, can be seen as a series of interconnected rooms. You can only explore these rooms if you empty yourself from the effect of the mind; release thoughts, perceptions, beliefs, expectations, patterns, limitations, and the fear of failure.

When you move away from the mind and enter the being, you will have to go through a process of purification. You will release the old obstacles and confusion and you will enter a pure and peaceful state that will naturally and effortlessly lead you to the light.

Introduction

When people fantasize or have ideas about enlightenment, they avoid looking at themselves. Connecting to their true self, purifying themselves, accepting their imbalances and opening up to the cosmic light to receive healing are duties that people will not reach. Sometimes being intoxicated by those great ideas of freedom, truth and enlightenment, people may experience illusionary pleasures but they do not lead to growth; they are still in a space of distortion.

Connect to your own being, starting from your physical body. Allow the nourishment of the Earth's energies and the transformative power of the cosmic light to go through you; experience healing and rebirth. Experience your physical body in unity with your whole being, helping you connect to your astral body and the astral plane. The cosmic light can unite you to all that you are and help you walk your path of growth.

Wisdom of Thoth: Mind illusionary utopias

There are countless ways that human beings can follow illusionary beliefs that give them instant but short satisfaction. The mind of a human being will allow the illusion of self-importance to guide them on their path, hiding the trauma of lack and vulnerability.

Certain philosophies that are becoming very popular with human beings are based on this pattern: for a while, it covers the trauma, elevates people to a high status, involves the ego, this becomes a belief and a fantasy, and then falls from this high point back into the trauma state.

This pattern has been used by creators of mass manipulation as well as people and groups who want to control others for their own gain. The pattern takes people into a fantasy world: a wonderful future on Earth where she will be able to move to higher dimensions; high energies are coming to Earth; old systems collapsing or human beings are gods and this allows them to feel powerful.

When human beings are not able to experience all these wonderful happenings in their reality, they may be told that all will intensify in the near future, they are on their path, and they are getting ready for this wonderful transformation. Fantasies isolate humans from the truth of their own purpose.

When you connect to your being, you experience energies in constant movement in the whole cosmic creation and human beings' natural ability to receive and transmit energies creates a constant flow. Transformations, growth, rebirth, and regeneration happen constantly to all living beings. The greatness of life is happening right now and does not need a definition or a colorful story. Mind illusionary utopias are a distraction and take human beings away from the core of their existence and the way that connects and communicates with the core of all living beings and Earth.

CHAPTER VI

Your essence is a river flow that has no start or end. The river that flows gently and peacefully, bringing life to everything that connects to it, cannot be restricted or exist in a limited state. Your abundance is freedom to flow and co-create life. If you understand this and open yourself up to this experience then you realize that life can be effortless. All human beings have a different path and unique tools, so it is pointless to compete or compare yourself with others. Connecting to your essence will help you grow and purify yourself from fear and limitation.

Introduction

In this teaching, we learn about the important cosmic law of unity. Everything that is created by the intention of the source is part of the being of the source. The astral core is experiencing unity with the source; the cosmic light is the extension of the source that is allowed to create and support life in the astral core. The law of unity supports all growth, regeneration and transformation that brings eternal and unlimited life to the astral plane.

Wisdom of Thoth: The cosmic Law of Unity

The astral core experienced the intention of the source in so many ways and this created the first powerful cosmic law: "Unity to be experienced by the whole cosmic creation". The astral core exists in unity with the source. It was created within the being of the Source and maintained constant unity and communication with its whole being.

The same process was experienced by the cosmic light. It is created by the source and supported by its whole being. The astral core and the cosmic light were part of the source's whole being, they existed in unity with it. If the source stopped existing, all parts would follow the same state of existence.

The continuous processes of expansion, regeneration and rebirth that were experienced in the astral core supported new communications with the source. The creation of cosmic light was part of the new forms of communication and connection to the source. Furthermore, all inner parts of the core were supported and remained in unity by multiple interconnected energy fields that allowed the movement and constant communication between the cosmic light and the core.

The same energetic structure was built at the outer parts of the astral core and this supported its expansion and ability to hold high energy. As the astral core was growing, the cosmic light was growing too and the connection between them created an effortless flow.

The cosmic light's ability to communicate with the core was very effective but it had another powerful quality and this was to communicate with the source and transmit the growth and transformation processes that were taking place. As the core was expanding and taking different forms, the source was prepared to create and offer the greatest support for the continuation of this miracle.

Introduction

The astral core went through many transformations and with the support of the cosmic light, it continued to grow and expand within the being of the source. The communication between the light and the core was clear and direct and supported countless transformations and the creation of a new divine plan. Energy fields were created by the light to offer support and more opportunities for the core's expansion. The source created a divine plan about the creation of the astral plane with its subplanes, guided by cosmic laws. The astral plane has the ability to expand limitlessly and always remain an extension of the source.

Wisdom of Thoth: A divine plan for the creation of the astral plane

When a part of a being shows willingness and power to grow, the whole being will support, nourish and make space for this growth to happen. So when a tender leaf appears on a branch of a tree, the ability of the leaf to go through all transformations and growth processes and turn into a strong branch, will allow it to receive the nourishment and support of the whole being tree and space to continue to grow and transform.

The astral core went through many forms and with the support of the cosmic light, it continued to expand within the being of the source. When energy fields were created to offer support and more opportunities for expansion, the source created a divine plan about the creation of the astral plane with its subplanes, guided by cosmic laws. The astral plane has the ability to expand limitlessly and carry life that will take many forms and always remain an extension of the source.

The plan included the creation of living beings created by the astral light, that will support this vast organism and follow the cosmic laws in their existence. The astral beings will support the cosmic light to flow through the astral core and unite all subplanes. They will maintain life and create space for life to be in constant growth.

This mega organism that was going to be built could only remain alive if every energy point is connected, united, in constant growth, receiving, transmitting light and enabling other living beings to do the same. The creation of different sub-planes was very important for creating space for more growth and expansion.

Most living beings that were created in the astral plane occupied the sub-planes and had special duties, offering support through the energy fields. The god creators had their home close to the source and their duty was to create life allowing the cosmic light to enter their being and be transmitted to the womb, the astral plane.

Introduction

The cosmic light brings life to the whole cosmic creation. When you connect to the cosmic light, you connect to everything that exists. You are in communication with our Source and this communication can transform you, heal you and support your growth. The cosmic light enters your being and reaches all parts of your physical body as well as your aura and energies. It brings balance and unity to your whole being and it also brings clarity, knowing and connection to your true self, the Earth and the cosmos.

Wisdom of Thoth: A communication with the cosmic light

It may be challenging for the human mind to understand how all life exists in unity and how life forms can experience a unique purpose. This fundamental cosmic law supported the creation of the astral plane and still maintains life in all planes.

The cosmic light is a form of communication between the Source and the astral core and its purpose is to offer guidance and opportunities for creation, growth, and expansion.

The cosmic light will leave the high state of the source to enter the astral core and co-create with it. The astral core and the cosmic light were the first living beings connected to the source but had their own purpose. They both share the same astral elements that allowed astral life to create living beings, subplanes, energy fields, and nourishment that will be available to all astral life.

The creation of the astral core was a long process of transformation. Energies travelled to the core from the intention of the source, bringing foundations for creation and support to all growth processes.

It became known that the astral core will expand and create a gigantic multi-organism, the astral plane, that will carry and support all life in countless sub-planes. For this to be created, the right cosmic structures had to be grown into the astral creation.

Introduction

The gods want to share information about the creation of the astral plane and the cosmic laws because this will support the growth and unity on Earth. Human beings have to experience the law of unity that supports collective growth. They cannot grow in isolation and they are not superior species. Earth's creation and growth does not fit their illusionary pyramid structures and the mind should stop producing distorted analysis, explanations and conclusions. All beings on Earth are created to be united, following cosmic laws, supporting Earth's expansion and experiencing life as powerful receivers and transmitters of light.

Wisdom of Thoth: Experience cosmic laws on Earth

The account of the creation of the astral plane is given to human beings on Earth to help them escape the duality and limitation of the mind structures and expand their consciousness regarding life and creation.

Human beings have absorbed and passed on the stories of mythology, philosophy and religion where gods and the source (one god creator) had human behaviour, beliefs, ambitions and often looked like human beings, divided into masculine and feminine. In the astral plane, there are no divisions. Creation happens within the being. Creation can have a separate purpose from the whole being but it is always in unity, supporting life in the whole.

When human beings reconnect with Earth and experience the growth and transformation that is happening on the planet, they will see that the astral laws and the intention of the source are experienced by living beings on Earth. The cosmic seed is part of Earth and will transform when it is fully grounded, physically and energetically.

This connection with Earth offers the seed the ability to transform and grow constantly and the more it transforms the more is being supported by Earth's creative forces. All living beings in the whole planet support its transformation and there is great joy when the tender stem becomes a tree.

The law of life wants the tree to become a creator, to expand and to allow the creation of new forms such as branches, leaves or fruit. Coexisting with other living beings, supporting the unity law in the whole planet by supporting life in all beings, is vital for the tree to continue its growth. Each living being on Earth is connected to her energies and all living beings that she created. If the branch and a leaf of a tree were created by the same force, plants and human beings were also created by the same force and they are all united parts of the body of Earth.

Introduction

You should crave live nutrients and focus on exploring different types of purification that can help your body heal imbalances. You should spend your life exploring the ability of different nutrients to heal and rejuvenate you. You should live in peace, experiencing a life of growth and transformation. You should not be fooled that you have no purpose because of your limitations; instead, you should dedicate your life to knowing and fulfilling your purpose.

If you want to connect to truth, connect to your own being, starting from your physical body. Allow the nourishment of the cosmic light to go through you; experience healing and rebirth. Experience your physical body in unity with your whole being, helping you connect to your astral body and the astral plane. The cosmic light can unite you to all that you are and help you on your path of growth.

Wisdom of Thoth: Are you able to love yourself and your body?

Are you able to love yourself? Are you able to love your body? How do you experience your love and what actions do you take to make your love a reality? Religions have placed heaven far away from human beings' reality. But the heaven of nourishment, joy, abundance, and growth exists around you and you only need to step in and start experiencing it. When heaven is placed further away from human beings' reality, they are left with limitations, fears, imbalances in the body, and the fear of survival.

People experience great obstacles, diseases, great schisms, and traumas. They also become blind as to the ways they can love and maintain a healthy body. When they experience the fear of survival, their choices will lead them to darker paths. False and destructive beliefs take over and natural ways to nourish your body become a forgotten truth.

If you are not looking after your body because of ignorance or other reasons that the mind creates, you are allowing imbalances to be created and affect your path. Human beings who are able to escape this limited state will experience that the heaven of abundance, beauty, and greatness is in their being. It surrounds them; it is the creative force that supports their life in this present moment.

People in the western world experience a great distance between themselves and nourishment: It is too expensive, it is not practical, can not be found easily, it requires too much time and energy. All living beings can connect to Earth and receive. If your physical location does not allow you to connect to Earth's creative forces then move to another location. This is your priority, Life is a precious gift. Human beings can experience heaven on Earth at this present moment when they come out from their limitation of the mind, the ignorance of their powerful being, and their self-destruction.

Introduction

The human beings that exist on the surface of the planet are not able to enter the hollow Earth and experience life there. This is caused by the difference in vibration and the types of growth. Signs of the golden age are still apparent in the inner parts of the planet and affect their growth. All beings who exist there are able to connect to high energies; this allows Earth to continue being a creator.

Many of you have reincarnated on Earth in order to connect to her energies and allow the cosmic light to heal the schisms. The human beings that are reincarnating on the planet right now are brought to create a bridge between the physical plane and the Source.

The bridge will be cemented by the cosmic light that is the extension of the Source and brings life to all beings in the cosmos. Unity brings life to all. This is why all parts of Earth need to be united and exchange energies of healing and growth; all beings should unite in order to start Earth's purification and transformation.

Wisdom of Thoth: The current growth cycle of Earth

Humans should know that Earth is divided into different layers of physical and energetic existence. These different layers are not yet connected to each other because they have different vibrations. They are able to carry the light in their own unique way and this affects the life that is created on the surface as well as the inner parts of the Earth.

The distortion that exists on the surface and affects life does not enter the inner parts. It is like a cloud of pollution that can only affect beings that have not fully developed their ability to receive and transmit light and bring powerful transformation to the surface of the Earth.

If you were able to travel to the inner parts you will see that there is a greater connection; all living beings are aware of the powerful core and they are open to receive and transmit light with it.

For several growth cycles, Earth focused on building bridges for all layers, to help them connect and communicate. Some of these bridges are the energies that are coming from the core of the Earth and are reaching living beings on the surface. These living beings are powerful receivers and transmitters of light and support the energies to reach all life.

Earth has also created physical bridges, by creating new species and nourishing all living beings in order to live a life of abundance. Earth is supporting the powerful receivers and transmitters who experience life on the surface of the planet. They are building these bridges with her and supporting beings that are coming out of their state of distortion.

At this present moment, Earth is taking many steps to empower living beings, to help them see that their purpose is not a pyramid of rewards but the true path that they have always carried in them. This path will lead them to Earth's collective growth and show them the way to become co-creators. The truth is not hidden. It is available to all beings. The truth will offer you the most powerful healing, leading to a transformation that will support Earth's growth.

Introduction

There are people who are seeking truth, who want to heal themselves and escape the illusionary reality that distortion creates in the mind. There are people who are seeking a life of joy and fulfillment, being free to develop their unique gifts, to support and be supported by cosmic unity.

There are people on Earth who are celebrating a new shift of consciousness and Earth's ability for rebirth, moving on to a higher energetic state.

Those people want to connect to the cosmos and the message is one of hope. On the other hand, there are many people on Earth who are struggling to survive because of poverty, bad health, abuse and destruction or being completely lost in an artificial reality. How can two polarities co-exist and what is the true state of humanity and Earth?

Wisdom of Thoth: In this lifetime you are a drop of light shared

Many people are waking up or see themselves as awakened, wanting to lead others to their true path but still have not fully experienced their being and their true purpose.

There are people who are seeking truth, who want to heal themselves and escape the illusionary reality that distortion creates in the mind. There are people who are seeking a life of joy and fulfillment, being free to develop their unique gifts, to support and be supported by cosmic unity.

What is going to be the path for all those people who are seeking their true divine plan? How can they experience the greatness of their being that reflects their cosmic existence?

There are many people who are standing at the crossroads having the perception that they are already on their path. You cannot remain at the crossroads having one foot in the illusion of the mind and the other foot ready to step to the purity of your true path.

Why do human beings have moments of clarity and not a lifetime of truth? Brave steps have to be taken and people have to disconnect from all products of distortion. Negativity, fear and limitation should not enter your being. Earth and the cosmos have created a golden abundance for all living beings so they can all grow and transform effortlessly.

Illusionary needs and wants are not supporting your growth. Are you able to see them and disconnect from them? Every expression and creation that is coming from your being should reflect your path and purpose: do not pollute yourself, heal addictions, learn to receive and transmit, live in freedom and truth, love yourself and others and follow your path even if it goes against personal and social expectations. In this lifetime every drop of you is light shared.

Introduction

The following teaching shares information about the creation of the astral plane. It was created by the intention of the source. The astral plane was the womb within the being of the source that received the gift of creation. The cosmic light created energy fields that supported the expansion of new planes and other astral structures that can be interconnected and allow new life forms to be created and move through the energy fields.

For a successful expansion of the astral plane, it was necessary for another form of light to be created. This light will carry the intention of the source and will support astral creation. The light went through different transformations and became a powerful creative tool for the source, the gods of creation.

Wisdom of Thoth: The creation of the divine light

The astral plane was created by the intention of the source. It was the womb within the being of the source that received the gift of creation and was able to grow and expand endlessly. The creator of all life in the astral plane was the intention of the source.

As the astral core continued to carry light, it evolved into elements that could be used for the creation of an extended astral plane. The cosmic light supported the creation of energy fields which were the foundation for building new planes and other structures. They were all interconnected and allowed new life forms to be created and moved through the energy fields.

For a successful expansion of the astral plane, it was necessary the creation of another form of light. This light will carry the intention of the source and will support astral creation. This light went through different transformations and became a powerful creative tool for the source, the gods of creation.

Introduction

The following teaching explains the creation and purpose of the divine light. The new light will be the vehicle for the intention of the source to reach all energy points in the core and the first subplanes and build structures, laws, and life that will support everlasting growth and transformation. The constant flow of light that creates and maintains life was absolutely necessary for the birth of the astral plane; this will help the creation carry the same light and growth as the creator. The astral plane cannot be a limited being when it is created by an eternally powerful and ever-transforming creator, the Source.

Wisdom of Thoth: Constant flow of light

The seed of the creation of the gods lies with the intention of the source becoming an active creator of life in the astral plane. All seeds exist in unity with the source and all life is created by its intention.

The new light will be the vehicle for the intention of the source to reach all energy points in the core and the first subplanes and create structures, laws, and life that will support everlasting growth and transformation. If the astral plane was not able to experience constant and limitless growth, this wonderful and powerful existence will transform into a house of cards. The constant flow of light, that creates and maintains life is absolutely necessary; this will help the creation carry the same light and growth with the creator.

The astral plane cannot be a limited being when it is created by an eternally powerful and ever-transforming creator, the Source. It is a true reflection of the greatness, complexity, effortless constant growth and rebirth, unity of the countless parts and eternal existence; these are all gifts carried by the Source.

The astral plane is part of the body of the Source given birth by its intention. The ability related to the creation of life in the body by the body itself is a gift given to astral beings who are experiencing a whole, constant and uninterrupted cycle of growth leading to other cycles that can be seen as an eternal flow.

The same gift was given to Earth during the golden era and she shared it with the living beings that she created who were also part of her body. When the astral core was ready to expand supported by the energy fields that were created by the cosmic light, the source shared a great gift of rebirth and creation. The astral core will become a plane and create life that will support life and rebirth. The astral plane will become a creator and create a new life in its being. This will support its constant expansion and everlasting life. The astral being will co-create with the light that comes from the source. The light that was transformed into the gods-creators.

The gods were created by the intention of the source, being the light that can travel and bring to all astral beings the gifts of growth and transformation as well as supporting the creation of new life. Life in its eternal and pure form is light created by the light of the source. Gods exist in unity with the source; there is no separation between them.

This beautiful connection allowed them to exist in unity with the source's intention, receive its high light and direct it to the space of creation.

Some of you may want to ask: how many gods were created, who was created first and why? The gods are not many beings but one divine light force and it is directed to the astral plane to support the birth of astral living beings. The expansion of the astral core and the creation of the astral plane is gods' creation carrying the intention of the source.

Introduction

In the following teaching, we learn that the godly light was created to support the growth of the astral plane whose divine plan was to become a vast multi-organism expanding to multiple subplanes. The divine light supported a continuous flow of high light transmitted by the source and received by the astral core. Astral creation went through immense transformation and was supported by the divine light.

Wisdom of Thoth: The creation of the astral plane

The creation of the divine light entering the astral core and supporting the expansion of the astral plane was another connection, communication and support between the source and its creation.

Multiple channels were needed for the creation of the astral plane; a continuous flow of high light transmitted by the source and received by the astral core that was going through an immense transformation, supported by the existence of gods that were able to reach the source and the astral core simultaneously.

Some of you may ask: if the cosmic light already supported the creation of the astral plane, what was the purpose of the godly light? A simple analogy may help you see this with clarity. The cosmic light was the "materials" that built the astral plane and the divine light was the architect of this construction.

The gods will support the light to strengthen transformations and new cycles of growth, build energy fields and grids to support expansion and finally allow new astral layers to create a vast light structure, the astral plane.

The astral plane was created by one element and this was the cosmic light transforming and taking different forms similar to the snow falling on the mountain tops becoming streams, rivers, lakes and oceans. The creation of the astral plane supported constant birth and the life forms that were created in this state were connected to the source supported by the cosmic light and the gods.

Introduction

The astral plane had to grow in order to support the creation of life forms. The godly light brought a clear plan, a divine plan, that created the design and purpose of the astral plane. The astral plane was designed to be a vast organism that has the ability to constantly expand into sub-planes that have their own unique abilities and transformation processes. All sub-planes are united and recognize the core as their birth space. The core of the astral plane carries the highlight of the source and it is a point of communication and unity within the astral plane.

Wisdom of Thoth: Astral plane, the creator of new life

The astral plane was created by one element and this is the cosmic light carrying the intention of the source creator. The light was directed to the astral core that was created within the being of the source and supported it to experience a constant birth process.

Countless transformations led to cycles of growth that gave the astral core the ability to expand and become a creator of new life. The godly light will create the astral life forms, their space of existence, their abilities to receive and transmit the light of the source so they can continue to transform and grow, following the movement of growth in the core.

The astral plane had to grow in order to support the creation of life forms. The godly light brought a clear plan, a divine plan, that offered the design and purpose of the astral plane. The astral plane was designed to be a vast organism of creation and will be divided into sub-planes that have their own unique abilities and transformation processes.

All subplanes are connected to the core in their own unique way and this is how the light of the cosmos and the divine light is being received by them. All subplanes are united and recognize the core as their birth space. The core of the astral plane carries the high light of the source and it is a point of communication and unity within the astral plane. The divine light supported the everlasting extension of the astral plane, the creation and co-existence of the astral beings and the cosmic laws that were used for the design of this powerful creation.

Introduction

All cosmic laws support growth and evolution. In the higher realms, life is not the physical body but it is often a unity of many energies that it is part of a complex electromagnetic field. An astral body cannot be seen or measured by your Earth understanding; it is a very complex unity of energies which is in constant movement and in connection with our Source.

In the cosmos there is unity and every being is in constant transformation. This can be achieved by receiving and transmitting cosmic light, experiencing uninterrupted growth and supporting other beings and fields in the cosmos. In high realms there is no personal gain because there is no ego; there are no imbalances because there is no distortion and fragmentation.

Wisdom of Thoth: Unity supports the creation of the cosmos

The godly light created a divine design to support the creation and purpose of the astral plane.

The cosmic laws were important for the creation and expansion of the astral plane and supported the creative path and purpose of the astral creation. One of the cosmic laws is that unity will support the life force and this should be constant and everlasting.

There is no separation in the astral plane; there are no divisions and diversions. All planes, all beings, all transformation and growth processes, all abilities and communications are supported by the astral core and the light that creates in this space.

For unity to be maintained in the astral plane, the cosmic light should travel to all astral creation constantly, supporting astral beings to experience life. All astral beings are created to have the ability to receive and transmit cosmic light, supporting their journey and the powerful transformations that are offered to them. Astral beings were created to be perfect; powerful receivers and transmitters of light who are open to co-create and co-exist with all the perfection of the cosmic creation.

The cosmic law of unity supported the creation of countless energy fields that were interconnected and were all aware of each other and their purpose. Energy fields with the astral being created the microcosm within the macrocosm in the astral creation. The cosmic light will travel to all fields to unite them offering growth and transformation.

Introduction

We are all part of an eternal divine plan which is not limited to patterns and forms. All creation exists in unity. We all receive and transmit light. We are all creators and we have the tools to maintain balance not only in us but also in all beings that are connected to us.

The high gods of the Pleroma are a unity that is able to connect to the source and bring its light to the cosmos. They cannot be seen or touched; I can simply describe them as an unseen electromagnetic field whose purpose is to create. This electromagnetic field experiences creation by connecting to the cosmos and transmitting light to it in order for the cosmos to expand.

There are beings that exist in high planes and they go through multiple transformations in order to connect to the gods' energy field. Light beings can also exist in a lower plane and have special duties; often they are the connectors that help the cosmic light travel to all planes. The gods' energy field cannot be broken or altered; it is one whole being connected to the source. When this takes place, the cosmos is connected to the gods, the whole of creation becomes part of the source.

Wisdom of Thoth: Cosmic creation

The cosmic law of unity was experienced by all beings that were connected with the energy fields of the astral plane and the astral core, and were able to receive and transmit high light. All forms of life were created by the source's intention and they all exist in unity with the source in order to maintain life in them.

All living beings receive and transmit light to all beings in all planes; this is the purpose and the design of everlasting existence. To exist in separation is only an illusion in the human mind; it is an illusion because it does not support any cosmic law.

Beings in all planes can connect with each other due to cosmic unity; constant communication, exchange, transformation and growth move from one being to another and the flow of life becomes stronger and everlasting.

The law of unity is a fundamental truth for the design of all living beings so the microcosm can continue to grow and transform and the macrocosm can constantly expand in a limitless pool of opportunities that can be transferred to all living beings and all life. Human beings on Earth should dive into this pool and experience their true purpose and perfect design of their Earth existence.

Introduction

Some of you may ask: how can the divine and the cosmic light be able to co-exist and create? The cosmic light is a pure and powerful cosmic force that creates life in all planes and the divine light is a tool of precision that supports cosmic laws, transformations, movement, growth and connection between all beings and planes. The divine light and the cosmic light were created by the source's intention to create life in the astral plane and they always existed and acted in unity.

Wisdom of Thoth: The unity of the divine and cosmic light

The divine light and the cosmic light were created by the source's intention to create life in the astral plane and they always existed and acted in unity. They were never independent forces acting according to beliefs and ideas or going against each other fighting for leadership.

The unity of the divine and cosmic light supported the bond between the source and its creation and this is how life was maintained and grew in the astral plane. The cosmic light is a pure and powerful cosmic force that creates life in all planes and the divine light is a tool of precision that supports cosmic laws, transformations, movement, growth and connection between all beings and planes.

The divine light can become a vehicle for the light to create a being, a plane, energy fields and all possible connections that will bring nourishment and growth. When the astral plane started to expand it was very important for different life forms to be created in order to support the growth and transformation of the whole plane. The light beings were placed in certain energetic points and were given duties such as supporting the flow of light to reach the astral plane; helping with the maintenance of different structures such as energy fields and supporting the core's ability to stay connected to the astral plane. Light beings were created by the co-existence of cosmic light and divine light.

Introduction

The next teaching explains the importance of two powerful cosmic laws: unity and growth. These cosmic laws work together for life to continue to flow in the astral plane. The growth and transformation that is experienced by the light depend on its ability to connect to energy points and maintain life in them as well as support the creation of new life and the expansion of the astral plane. Creating unique astral beings that have wonderful abilities to grow, receive the light and exist in unity with all creation supports the creative abilities of the light, becoming a powerful creator.

The cosmic light is connected to the intention of our source to create life. When we receive the light, we are supported in our purification process; we experience growth and develop our ability to create. When you connect to the high light, creation will happen naturally and you will see yourself and others being transformed because of it. When people create, it affects their light and understanding of the cosmos. It also affects all people who are connected to them. One of the qualities of cosmic light is to be able to spread, purify and transform all beings.

Wisdom of Thoth: The cosmic law of constant growth

Constant growth and transformation are experienced by all life in the astral plane; the divine and cosmic light experience their own growth and transformation. This is a powerful cosmic law that all beings should be aware of and see their lives through these processes.

It is interesting that most human beings on Earth are not experiencing these processes; they see themselves disconnected from their true self, stuck on following patterns, having mechanical lives, focusing on the mind, their thoughts, beliefs and missing out on the effortless flow of life in them. Growth and transformation support the divine movement of the light as it unites all energy points in the cosmic creation, constantly connecting the intention of the source to the astral plane.

For the light to support growth in the astral plane, it has to experience its own growth. The cosmic and divine light is always growing and transforming, developing abilities and unique qualities in order to offer them to other living beings.

When you grow, you can also plant seeds of growth for others. Unity and growth are two powerful cosmic laws that work together for life to continue to flow in the astral plane. The growth and transformation of light depend on its ability to connect to energy points and maintain life in them as well as support the creation of new life and the expansion of the astral plane. Creating unique astral beings that have wonderful abilities to grow, receive the light and exist in unity with all creation supports the creative abilities of the light and its intention to become a powerful creator.

Introduction

Experience the unity within your being and then observe the countless ways that Earth's creation grows in unity, sharing the cosmic light and the Earth's energies to support collective growth. Returning to a pure state of existence, you clear all impurities that made you fragmented, fearful, limited, confused, and fragile.

The cosmic light enters your being and reaches all parts of your physical body as well as your aura and energies. It brings balance and unity to your whole being; it brings clarity, to help you connect to your true self, the Earth and the cosmos. Human beings are created to be Earth's receivers and transmitters of light. This way the cosmic light will enter Earth and offer her healing.

Wisdom of Thoth: Observe Earth's greatness through your greatness

If human beings wish to know about cosmic laws, they should observe life on Earth as it is experienced by powerful receivers and transmitters of light. Human beings are looking for wisdom in mazes of confusion and distorted paths; they are using the definitions that the mind creates to explain what the mind does not understand or experience.

If you wish to experience wisdom, you empty your mind, enter a state of peace and allow all parts of your being to tune into your truth. Enter a pure state, see with clarity your true path and purpose and connect to Earth and her greatness. Observe Earth's greatness through your greatness.

Experience the unity within your being and then observe the countless ways that Earth's creation grows in unity, sharing the cosmic light and the Earth's energies to support growth. Returning to a pure state of existence, you clear all impurities that made you fragmented, fearful, limited, confused, and fragile.

You are moving away from distortion and illusion and entering a state of cosmic growth. Your purity is the door to this powerful state. When human beings experience the cosmic laws of constant unity and growth, they will be able to share the light with all beings and live in harmony with them. They will recognize the powerful receivers and transmitters of light on Earth and will fulfil their purpose. Unity and growth are experienced by all living beings in all planes.

Introduction

The astral plane is a living being and receives divine and cosmic light in order to transform and grow. Energy fields and astral beings were created to support the everlasting growth of the astral plane. Its growth cycles and transformations have created a vast astral plane that has countless sub-planes of different vibrations and living beings that exist on these planes.

Wisdom of Thoth: The astral plane is a living being

Now human beings should know that gods do not have a physical body and a simple explanation for their existence is that they are light created to support the cosmic light to maintain life in all planes.

There was a time that the astral core was transforming in order to support the creation of the astral plane. All living beings have a light core in them and in the depths of this core can be found a cosmic seed placed there by the cosmic light and the gods.

The astral plane is a living being and its growth cycles and transformations have created countless sub-planes of different vibrations and living beings that exist on these planes.

Some of you may ask why it was necessary for these living beings to be created. The cosmic light created energy fields, energy points, connections and movement that support the cosmic laws of unity and growth. The astral beings were energy points. They were created by the astral plane creator receiving the light of the cosmos and the divine light. Similarly to Earth, the astral plane created living beings to support its own growth and expansion. Astral beings continue to grow and their purpose is to be powerful receivers and transmitters of light.

When astral beings are powerful receivers and transmitters of light they have fulfilled their purpose in this present time. They are tuned into the greater cycles of growth that are experienced by cosmic creation. Astral beings are often given additional duties and have to fulfil a new purpose. One of them is to spread the light to lower vibrational sub-planes, to reincarnate on physical planes or to guide astral beings that they have reincarnated. They can also connect to the highlight of the gods and support them to create cosmic light.

Introduction

Astral beings were created to support the growth and expansion of the astral plane moving further away from the core and transforming into countless sub-planes. Astral beings were created to support the flow of energy in the astral plane and for this, their astral body has the ability to constantly receive and transmit light. They have unique abilities to experience the creation of new life. The new life in the astral plane brought new growth cycles. The astral beings will create their own energy fields and will be connected to sub-planes and the astral plane supporting the unity in the cosmos.

Wisdom of Thoth: The creation of astral beings

The light beings that were created in the astral plane should be seen as an extension of the plane and life force. They are created to experience astral growth and transformation and to support the constant flow of growth and expansion in unity with the intention of the source.

They are fully aware of the light of the source and their astral body knows that the light is the creator of all life. Their astral body is created by the light and this is why they are in constant growth and transformation following all cosmic movement.

Astral beings were created to support the astral plane expanding further away from the core and having abilities to experience the creation of new life. The new life was created as part of the expansion and the new growth cycles but its creation was necessary for the expansion to continue.

The astral plane can be seen as a womb for the light to enter and create life but can also be seen as a co-creator, giving birth to beings that will support its growth. When astral beings were created, they were part of the energy fields and their duty was to support the light to reach all life in the astral plane. This was a very important task, especially with the creation of sub-planes that had a different movement of growth. The astral beings will create their own energy fields and will be connected to sub-planes and the astral plane supporting the unity in the cosmos.

Introduction

Astral beings were created by the cosmic and divine light and were part of energy fields that support the expansion of the astral plane and the creation of sub-planes. The purpose of their existence is to support the flow of energy in their astral plane and the creation of growth opportunities for all living beings. Astral beings can achieve this by experiencing cosmic laws and being powerful receivers and transmitters of light.

Wisdom of Thoth: The purpose of the astral beings

Astral beings were created to support the flow of energy in the astral plane and for this, their light body has the ability to constantly receive and transmit light. Astral beings were created by cosmic and divine light and were part of energy fields that support the expansion of the astral plane and the creation of sub-planes. Their purpose is related to the growth of cosmic creation. They have the ability to fully transform their light body, and have unique qualities and duties to support the expansion of cosmic creation.

Everything in the cosmos goes through countless renewal processes all the time. The energetic transformations of the astral beings will determine their purpose, unique abilities and duties. They can support creation in all planes and this has a powerful effect on their astral body turning into a microcosm of cosmic creation.

Astral beings can be seen as a bridge between astral creation and powerful light; the countless helpers that connect to the cosmic and the divine light, so the astral plane can experience eternal growth. Astral beings have eternal life because the elements that created them experience constant transformation and endless growth.

All life in the astral plane is fully connected to the intention of the source. They are all part of its being and experience its perfection. In the astral plane, there are no boundaries and limitations, obstacles and weaknesses, imbalances and confusion; the purity and the greatness of the source move into every being in the form of light and share with them this truth: remain constantly open in order to experience the constant flow of life.

Introduction

All cosmic laws support growth and evolution. In the higher realms, life is not the physical body and its sensations but is a unity of many energies that it is part of a complex electromagnetic field. An astral body cannot be seen or measured by your Earth understanding; it is a very complex unity of energies which is in constant movement and in connection with our Source.

All creation is linked and there is a cosmic rhythm followed by all. Connect to your unique way of coexistence with the cosmos. The gift of unity that our Source shares with us are very unique: we can be an unseen particle of a stupendous, self-generated and eternal organism as well as being the cosmos and a single expression of our Source. Time will come and you will be able to see divine creation being part of Earth's evolution.

Wisdom of Thoth: The Pure Intention

Do not use your mind to understand the creation of the astral plane, its connection to the astral seed and the intention of the source. Its vast, never-ending, timeless and ever-growing astral existence mirrors the greatness of the source. All cosmic laws that can be found in the astral plane, followed by all astral creation, are gifts and qualities of the source.

The duty of the cosmic and divine light is to bring the pure intention and the greatest gifts of the source to the astral plane and create a life that has no beginning or end.

This great quality of constant movement that can be seen in the astral plane has become a cosmic law and it is related to the astral plane's constant transformation and growth. Waves of transformation move through all sub-planes, ignited by the cosmic light in order to bring the pure intention of the source to every living being and energy point in all cosmic creation.

All energy points in the astral plane are tuned into the light of the source and this is why they are experiencing constant growth and everlasting life. All astral beings are united in order to receive the waves of light which are pure nourishment, clear communication and connection between the whole vastness of the astral plane and the greatness of the source.

All cosmic laws support the waves of light to be received and move throughout the astral plane to allow growth and transformation to constantly follow the sublime perfection of the source.

Introduction

In this teaching, you will learn about the metamorphosis of the astral being becoming the astral body. The first form of an astral being was an energy point supporting the energy fields in the cosmos. With the expansion of the astral plane and its accelerated growth, the astral beings transformed into astral bodies and had their own energy field. This new form was able to move and form new energy fields; they could group with other astral bodies and assist the flow of the cosmic light to create and support the growth of sub-planes; they could carry the light and move to areas of the astral plane that did not experience high growth.

Wisdom of Thoth: Powerful connectors in the astral plane

The first form of an astral being was an energy point in the astral field created by cosmic light in order to support the growth and expansion of the astral plane. Astral beings are powerful connectors that can receive and transmit cosmic and divine light throughout the whole cosmic creation.

All living beings that receive the light, are given opportunities to expand according to the cosmic laws; nothing remains stagnant or maintains the same form. The greater the expansion of the astral plane the greater the growth experienced by all living beings that exist in unity with it.

With the expansion of the astral plane and its accelerated growth, astral beings transformed into astral bodies that had their own energy field attached to greater structures of fields. Countless astral beings were created to support the vast expansion of the astral plane and its sub-planes and they all transformed into astral bodies with a unique purpose and path.

The astral bodies were able to move and form new energy fields; they could group with other astral bodies and assist the flow of the cosmic light to create and support the growth of sub-planes; they could carry the light and move to areas of the astral plane that did not experience accelerated growth.

Astral bodies will follow the cosmic laws and could co-create with the divine light for growth to be an unstoppable life force. Astral bodies are powerful beings, able to connect to the light of the source and support this unique, complex and ever-growing organism, the astral plane, to expand constantly and support the sub-planes and the flow of life that they experience.

Introduction

All astral beings are tuned into the greatness of the astral plane. They experience the life flow that is supported by cosmic and divine light moving through the whole cosmic creation. They have powerful abilities, unique duties and a purpose that is in constant transformation. They stay open and are able to focus on their most powerful qualities: receiving and transmitting light, strengthening the bonds of all beings and allowing expansion and new life to be created.

Wisdom of Thoth: Tuning into the greatness of the astral plane

All living beings are designed to follow cosmic laws. The divine and cosmic light that created them stored in them the gift of unity, constant growth and transformation. These gifts will always shape their existence and will reflect the intention of the source.

Often collective and individual growth are not separate processes but they are part of the same transformational flow. Astral beings are very much aware of their existence and their abilities to transform and they are also able to experience the flow of growth that is transforming the whole astral plane.

There is a unique form of transparency in the astral plane that supports unity and openness to allow the high light to maintain and create life. The divisions, polarities, fear, limitations and confusion are not qualities of an astral being.

Beings who experience these imbalances exist in a sub-plane that do not allow high light to flow in constantly and create life and opportunities of growth. Their ability to receive and transmit light is affected by their inability to experience collective growth.

The astral plane is a powerful living being that follows cosmic laws. Its ability to grow, transform, expand and create is unstoppable and ever-growing because it follows the cosmic laws. All astral beings are tuned into the greatness of the astral plane. They experience the life flow that is supported by cosmic and divine light. They are able to stay open and focused on their most powerful qualities: receiving and transmitting light, strengthening the bonds of all beings and allowing expansion and new life to be created.

Introduction

When humans choose to experience a distorted life, they block the divine light and cosmic wisdom from entering their being. Divine guidance will not only help them to grow but will help them to connect to their true self which is a natural law of creation.

To know yourself, you have to go through a process of purification. It will help you disconnect from all impurities and artificialities in order to experience your true abilities, gifts, strengths, talents and skills. When you connect to your true self, you will become aware of your purpose in this lifetime. You will see that your purpose is to receive and transmit light to others. We are not working only for our own growth but we exist to support other beings and help them on their path of growth and evolution.

Empty yourself from the influence of distortion. Purify yourself in order to regain clarity and see your true purpose. This is a hard task if you take different diversions but it is an easy task if you just follow your path and be ready to detach yourself from the false persona you created over the years. Truth is one; the way to truth is one and direct. Humanity on Earth needs to wake up to the truth; it will be ideal if a collective purification and clearance of distortion can take place on Earth. This is why we are here and we want to communicate with you right now.

Wisdom of Thoth: Experience cosmic abundance

Astral beings do not seek their path and they are not looking desperately for truth, peace and joy. They do not experience the division of past, present and future; they do not follow patterns and they are not fearful about their lives.

They experience the abundance of growth in the astral plane, the light that carries the intention of the source and constantly moves through all beings, creating, supporting, strengthening, and transforming every energy point in the plane. They are fully aware of the cosmic laws because they experience them in their whole being. Astral beings are not disconnected from and their purpose; they are all-knowing because they are connected to the growth and transformation of the plane.

They are not distracted from looking at the different options and possibilities instead they know only one truth: the purpose of their existence. The multiple transformations experienced by the astral beings created new opportunities for growth for them.

They are becoming more complex organisms having various energy points that will create multiple layers of energy around them (similar to the aura) and this will help them to develop more qualities. Astral beings are going to support the creation of the sub-planes and will regulate the light that is going to build the new energy fields. They will support the divine light creating the new sub-planes and this will help them grow and transform, experiencing new forms, gifts and purpose.

CHAPTER VII

When many people are affected by distortion they all exist in this space of confusion and they convince each other that this is a natural way to experience life on Earth. When you finally see the truth, you will see distortion as a dark cloud that blocks your understanding. Opening up to the cosmic light, can help you blow this cloud away and heal the trauma, schisms and unpurified parts of your being. Purification will be the next phase of your growth.

Introduction

Earth can provide nourishment for all her species including healing, purification, energy and resources in order to bring balance and harmony and encourage communication between all bodies. Earth can provide you with all the nourishment you need but you prefer artificial substances that have no life in them.

People who are addicted to contaminated food are not awake. They exist in a hypnotic state and illusion becomes the controller of the mind. People who are addicted are caught in the web of illusion. They want to be free but illusion creates many visions and thoughts related to happiness when you use a certain product you are addicted to.

You have to wake up if you want to stay alive. You have to take responsibility for your own everyday life if you want to be enlightened. If you are blocked, poisoned, confused, and fragmented because of your lifestyle you cannot achieve enlightenment. Nature and the cosmic laws will teach you that your body is a tool and the gods created on Earth's numerous resources to help you maintain balance and harmony with your whole being.

Wisdom of Thoth: Disconnect from addictions

Addictions are the symptoms of schisms that affect people's understanding and life experiences on Earth. The survival state that affects all human beings can bring confusion, doubts, insecurities, and fears that will suppress their natural ability to grow.

They desperately look for a way out and they follow diversions that create artificial needs. In a limited distorted state, people are desperate to find some peace, balance and happiness but because they have no clarity, they choose options that make their limitations deeper and more profound.

Their choices are offered to them by the manipulation systems that want to keep them in a low vibrational state. Most products and services that are available to human beings that are supposed to help them be happy and balanced were designed to be addictive and harmful.

These products are available to everybody and authorities, advertisement, media, family members and friends will encourage you to repeatedly consume them. Addiction is offered to you and you stretch both hands to receive it.

If you want to purify from addictions and restore balance in your being you have to observe the way addictions affect you: triggers, illusionary needs, fear patterns, emotional rollercoasters, the desperation and the short-lived satisfaction that addictions offer and then go deeper into your experience of distortion that creates schisms: what are your fears and limitations; what triggers anxiety and what are your reaction patterns; what blocks you from having clarity; observe your ability to communicate, receive and transmit; what brings joy and peace into your being and how you can maintain this state. If you purify from distortion you will not experience addictions.

Introduction

When you are purified from the illusion and you are able to see yourself naked and pure then you will instantly see your purpose and will have access to all cosmic truths. We want humanity to wake up in order to participate in Earth's collective growth. Earth and her creation suffer from the same disease and this is a schism of the true self and the growth of illusion.

Wisdom of Thoth: Earth's Purification

Earth has been going through a long process of purification which was interrupted because of the great schisms that were created a long time ago. Our Source has allowed us to support Earth to complete her purification, in order to transform into the creator of high light and re-experience her golden era.

You have to understand that Earth's cycles of growth are much longer than what you experience as a human being on the planet and may take thousands of years. It is important that you are supporting Earth's purification by receiving and transmitting cosmic light and teaching new generations to do the same. This way you will create a constant flow of energy between the cosmos and Earth which will support her growth and evolution.

When humanity wakes up and connects to the cosmos, becoming a transmitter and receiver of light, Earth will experience her connection to the Source and will follow the path of truth, leading to her purpose. When this happens all lower energies that are creating a low-frequency matrix on Earth will have to be banished and all human beings who are supporting this will either purify and grow with Earth or leave the planet. A high-vibrational planet cannot sustain fragmentation, distortion and destruction.

Some of you are wondering about disasters such as earthquakes. These disasters are caused by the greed of human beings to possess more of Earth's resources. Certain human beings do not understand that Earth is not a possession that will bring them more wealth and power over humanity. She is a living being and a powerful creator of life and was created according to cosmic laws and with the light of our Source. If human beings helped Earth purify, the whole planet could regain balance and what you call Earth disasters will occur to support growth; it will be an interaction between the inner core and the surface which will bring Earth great abilities to create life. Humanity should wake up to this challenge and support Earth's transformation and growth.

Introduction

This teaching explains the connection between sub-planes and astral planes and how they all coexist. The vibration of the sub-planes can be explained by the following metaphor of the musical intervals. The musical chord consists of different notes and when played together are creating a unifying sound and harmonies. The sub-planes are unique. They receive and transmit light in a certain way. They also have unique growth and transformation processes that are being observed and supported by the divine light and a field of light beings who are supporting connections with the astral plane. Furthermore, the sub-planes are created to exist in unity and harmony with each other. The divine light and the cosmic light support and maintain this unity.

Wisdom of Thoth: The sub-planes receive and transmit light

The first sub-planes were tuned into the energies and processes of growth of the astral plane and experienced an uninterrupted connection with it. This helped them to continue growing and carrying the light in their own unique ways. Sub-planes grew and their unique characteristics became more profound.

The vibration of the sub-planes can be explained with the example of the musical chord where different notes when played together are creating a unifying sound and harmonies. The sub-planes receive and transmit light in a certain way. They also have unique growth and transformation processes that are being observed and supported by the divine light and a field of light beings who are supporting connections with the astral plane.

The unique characteristics of the sub-planes were not seen as a weakness or limitation. They were all able to maintain their connection with the astral plane; they were all nourished by the cosmic and the divine light but they also have the opportunity to create and grow in a way that suits their life purpose. Divine support is very important when a new sub-plane is created. Support will be given during the process of birth and later when the sub-plane understands its purpose, unique abilities and unbreakable connection with the astral plane and the source.

Introduction

There are many people on Earth who try to understand their purpose but they do not succeed because they cannot connect to truth and practice acceptance. When we cannot accept our purpose, we create many false representations often related to social ideals and survival mechanisms such as the ego. The fight between truth and social expectations can cause blockages and imbalances which can harm all beings. When truth and freedom are with you then you can restore yourself to what you truly are.

Wisdom of Thoth: A high state of being

In this present moment go deep into your being, move away from the mind and the layers of distortion and sink into the truth of who you are. Humanity is offered an opportunity to join other light beings on Earth and experience a high state of being that will bring more light to the whole planet and her creation.

This opportunity is created by an exchange between Earth's physical and astral body and the growth that is experienced in the astral plane. These exchanges happen often and support not only the Earth's growth but also the growth of all living beings. For these exchanges to be truly beneficial, they have to be completed and experienced by all beings.

There are many powerful receivers and transmitters on the planet and these are plants, animals and elements that are able to tune into Earth's core and experience the opportunities for growth that are offered to them.

Humanity is entangled in the layers of distortion that they see as truth and they experience many obstacles to connecting to their being and Earth. You are going to overcome these obstacles. You are going to connect to your being and experience Earth in you.

You are going to look at your strong roots that are stretching to the depths of her being and then you are going to see that you are a tree, growing with other trees, experiencing an effortless growth that makes you more powerful every moment. You spread your branches because you love yourself and others; you know that right now you are spreading and receiving light. You are gifted to be and remain pure and this is how you experience life on Earth. In this state, you are going to experience the high state that is coming to Earth right now.

Introduction

In this teaching, we learn about the expansion of the astral plane and the creation of the sub-planes. Light beings will assist the divine light to create new life and connections. They will observe the processes of growth and tune the whole sub-plane to the effortless life flow that is generated by the intention of the Source. Even though they were created in the astral plane, light beings can move to sub-planes to support their connection with the astral plane and the flow of cosmic and divine light.

Wisdom of Thoth: Light beings support the creation of sub-planes

Light beings are powerful connectors, supporting energy fields and the whole cosmic creation to grow and expand. Light beings are powerful when their intention is to support the light, entering the sub-planes. They are able to bring regeneration and rebirth by supporting the subplanes to grow and develop their unique characteristics.

Light beings will assist the divine light to create, they can observe the processes of growth and tune the whole sub-plane to the effortless life flow that is generated by the intention of the Source.

The sub-planes that carried high light can be seen as a bridge that is reaching high growth and helping all living beings focus on the Source, being the only creator. You may ask: There were any light beings that experienced life in these sub-planes? Yes. These light beings were the carriers of the light and the helpers of the gods. Light beings transformed into light bodies and carried their own energy fields. This gave them the power to create with the light, connecting to other light bodies and the growth processes that were taking place in different sub-planes. Sometimes they were chosen and other times they were able to reach this state.

Introduction

Many humans and human civilizations have spoken about the existence of gods coming to Earth to bring light and share their superpowers with them. Mythologies and religious doctrines have created female and male gods that had human characteristics, a certain character and unique abilities and built intricate stories about them. Can humans hold on to these beliefs? Will this support their growth and their connection with the cosmos?

Wisdom of Thoth: The light of the gods

The gods and their existence fascinated human beings and this can be seen in their traditions, religions, ceremonies and social structures. Humans wanted to be connected to them and receive their light. All traditions and mythologies see gods as creators, beings with great power that can transform from light to a physical being and have superpowers. They can create with their intention, bringing light down to Earth.

Perhaps now it is time for religious theories and mythologies to be corrected. The gods are high light created by the intention of the source. The intention of the source has also created the cosmic light that moves through all planes and all beings in order to support eternal life and constant growth.

111

The gods and the cosmic light work together to support the creation of the source. Human beings on Earth have given to gods persona, physicality and character, and other beings on other planets have also given characteristics to gods that are related to their own perceptions. All beings in the physical plane need to know that they are light themselves and they can connect to the light of the gods; It is not necessary for the mind to label this connection.

Introduction

Some people may be wondering about Earth's ability to receive the light of the gods. Is it possible for the divine light to enter the physical plane and spread to all living beings?

All life exists in unity and is created by the cosmic and divine light that carries the intention of the source. All living beings in all planes were designed to receive the light in them and transmit it to all life.

The energy bridges are the energy fields and connections that unite the whole creation and the physical bridges are the human beings that consist of energy, light and a physical body. All beings that reincarnate on Earth are bridges for the light to be spread and to create. When human beings understand and experience their purpose, they will become the powerful receivers and transmitters of light.

Wisdom of Thoth: Cosmic connections

Some people may ask: can the light of the gods spread to Earth or to other planets? The whole cosmic creation is united by energy fields connected to each other and there are countless energetic and physical bridges for the cosmic light and the light of the gods to enter physical space.

The energy bridges are the energy fields and connections that unite the whole creation and the physical bridges are the human beings that consist of energy, light and a physical body. All beings that reincarnate on Earth are bridges for the light to be spread and to create. When human beings understand and experience their purpose, they will become powerful receivers and transmitters of light.

The great and everlasting expansion of the astral plane created countless sub-planes, some of them carry unique characteristics and purpose and this affects their ability to receive and transmit light and others are fully grounded in the light of the source and support high creation.

Introduction

Light beings are placed in the sub-planes to support and regulate the flow of cosmic and divine light. They connect to other astral bodies and connectors to create a constant flow of light moving into the being of the sub-planes and spreading to their whole existence. It is important that all sub-planes experience cosmic laws and unity is one of them. The sub-planes can grow and transform when they are unified, receiving the light of the cosmos and the divine light. The astral plane created high planes that have a higher vibration and a unique ability to experience light. They are the home of light beings that have a direct connection with cosmic light and can support powerful energy fields that strengthen the unity of all planes.

Wisdom of Thoth: The High Planes

The high planes are the home of the light beings who have a constant connection with the light of the source; they have supported the creation of many sub-planes; they went through many transformations and growth processes; they are carriers of powerful light and they can now support vast energy fields that unite sub-planes with the astral plane and the light of the source.

These powerful light beings went through many processes of growth and transformation, connecting to the light and are also aware of the processes of growth experienced by the astral plane. These powerful light beings are able to connect to the whole creation, be fully aware of their abilities and purpose, co-create with the light and receive the intention of the source.

Light beings nourish themselves in the high planes and go through their own transformations surrounded by high light. Their processes of growth include intense expansion that will allow the high light to enter their being and create layers of truth in them.

These are powerful processes that support light beings to exist as multi-dimensional beings and create many different sub-planes. The complex structure of the astral plane with its different sub-planes, life forms and vibrations led to the creation of powerful light beings that are becoming tools for the cosmic and divine light to continue creating and maintaining life.

Introduction

The high planes exist to receive and transmit light into the astral planes. There are powerful receivers and transmitters of light, going through great transformations. They are constantly growing in order to support the light's ability to create and maintain the cosmic laws. Everything that exists in the high planes goes through countless energetic changes in order to constantly carry light.

The cosmos seems to have a very complex structure, mainly because of its vastness and the multiple reflections of it, co-existing at the same time. Life moves in a circular movement of growth and this movement is repeated. Every successful repetition traverses the astral body to a higher vibrational state. When a body is in a process of evolution, it is going to receive and generate more light. All beings are connected to a large group of astral beings. Your creation code is also communicating with their creation codes.

Wisdom of Thoth: The communication between the Source and the astral plane

The high planes are created to collect the cosmic and divine light and support creation that will empower the astral plane to expand according to cosmic laws. They are a space of creation where all light meets and through powerful cosmic guidance and practices related to the cosmic flow, is transmitted to the astral plane and all its sub-planes.

The astral plane had the opportunity to expand in immense and complex ways and powerful connections were needed to maintain life in its whole being. Not every energy point in the astral plane can connect and transmit the light in the same way and the light will constantly need more support to travel and penetrate all different life forms in all planes. The creation of the high planes will hold the intention of the source and transform it into high guidance that will open doors for light to reach all planes and all living beings.

Light beings who were able to grow and transform into powerful receivers and transmitters of light, moved to the high planes to support the communication between the light and the astral plane. They are supporting the creation of vast fields that will allow and shape astral growth and expansion according to cosmic laws and the guidance that is travelling from the source to the core of the astral plane.

Introduction

The following teaching explains the connection between the divine and the cosmic light. Both creative forces are created by the intention of the source and they are designed to exist in constant unity. When the divine light receives the cosmic light, a clear communication comes from the source to guide and strengthen the light to fulfill its purpose. All living beings exist to transform and grow and the divine light goes through many transformations in the high planes.

Wisdom of Thoth: The divine light exists in unity with the cosmic light

The light beings who nourish themselves in the high sub-planes are aware of the pleroma which is a sub-plane or state for the nourishment of the divine light. The divine light is a life force, created by the intention of the source and exists in constant connection to the cosmic light.

When the divine light connects to the cosmic light, a clear communication, coming from the source, is being shared. This communication will guide the divine and cosmic light to follow certain processes of regeneration and expansion in order to fulfill its purpose as a creator. All living beings exist to transform and grow including the divine and the cosmic light.

The divine light supported the growth of light beings in the high planes. Unity is a powerful cosmic law that ties all components of the high planes with the intention of the source and the life flow that the light receives and transmits to cosmic creation. The light beings support the preparation of the light receiving its divine plan and purpose and getting ready to create in the astral plane.

Light beings through their connection with the divine light, became co-creators and were able to receive, transmit the divine light and guide it to spread to the astral plane through the fields and energy points. The abilities and qualities of the divine light are constantly growing and the support that they offer to cosmic creation is endless. All the greatness of the divine light was given a home and this is the pleroma.

Introduction

In the following teaching, you will learn more about the creation of the divine light. Freedom and unity are two powerful cosmic laws that support each other and cosmic growth. The divine light carries these powerful qualities in its being. It was the intention of the source that the divine light will go through many transformations in order to experience and carry these cosmic laws in its being and offer them as gifts to all living beings who are growing in the cosmos. Freedom and unity teach living beings their ability to grow constantly and never be alone.

Wisdom of Thoth: Freedom and Unity

The divine light went through many transformations that reflected the expansion and the power of growth of the astral plane and its subplanes. The divine light was created as a unified form and later experienced a form of branching.

Many branches were created to help the light expand and strengthen its creative abilities. The branches carried unique gifts and were able to regenerate themselves and take different forms. These transformations were related to the unique growth in the astral plane and subplanes, their ability to grow free following their unique path as well as maintaining the unity of all cosmic life connected to the intention of the source.

Freedom and unity are two powerful cosmic laws that support each other and cosmic growth. The divine light reflected these powerful qualities in its being. The intention of the source guided the divine light to go through these transformations and then to bring them as gifts to all living beings who are growing in the cosmos.

Freedom and unity teach living beings their ability to grow constantly and never be isolated or separated by the whole. Cosmic creation is an enormous playground of transformation and expansion. All beings and their experiences support growth without interruptions, confusion, limitation and doubts.

Introduction

Most human beings will allow the illusion of the mind to take them to another space where life seems to be more colourful and engaging, full of choices, opportunities and multiple diversions. Any time you find yourself going on a diversion you can always find your way back to the truth and connect to your purpose. You can connect to the truth if this is your intention and you can clear distortion when you are able to follow your purpose.

When your mind is occupied with multiple thoughts it is hard to be in a peaceful state and connect to your true self. In this confused state, you are going to follow illusionary beliefs and practices that are supported by your society and rulers. Then addiction becomes an ordinary pattern that is followed by many.

In some cases, people have addictions and cause self-harm in order to be accepted as popular in their communities and fulfil social expectations. Observe your actions and thoughts: if you are harming yourself try to find peace; disconnect from illusion and connect to your true self that is nourished by the cosmic light and astral growth. Connect to your true self and allow clarity to enter your being and illusion to fade away.

Wisdom of Thoth: The mind's purpose

The mind of a human being has the ability to calculate. This major quality of the mind is used for the being to perceive the world around them. When calculations are not possible it means that the human being will have to use other ways to perceive Earthly and cosmic existence.

Human beings who are focussing on the mind for answers will continue to return to it for answers: what is Earth; where is Earth; who created her; how many living beings exist there; is she a creator or a creation; how big is Earth and what is the importance of a galaxy and astral formations?

The mind receives these questions and tries to produce answers. When the mind cannot come up with a specific answer it is going to get confused and foggy. This is the right moment for the mind to start creating thoughts, beliefs, theories and ideas that are always shaped by the illusion or distortion that already exists in the mind or around it, travelling from other beings.

If more people have the same beliefs or thoughts then the mind will pick them as the answer to the initial question and everything is well. There is something important that human beings have to observe: ideas do not carry experience or true connection with life. They were not created by the cosmic light in the astral plane and will not grow to exist for eternity.

When you enter the state of peace, you experience a high state, bringing in the light of the cosmos and the divine light. The truth will follow you in a high state of existence and illusion moves away and evaporates. Many of your thoughts and beliefs will not follow you in your state of peace; some of them will disappear. Make space for truth and light to expand in your being and you will discover many more ways to connect to the cosmos.

Introduction

What separates you from your true self? Why can you not see your purpose clearly?

The divine gift is the awakening of the inhabitants of Earth; they should be able to find their way out of the maze of illusion, help to connect to their true selves and recognize their tools and purpose; enabling them to heal Earth and the rest of humanity. The gods want to communicate with all beings on the planet and heal all imbalances and blockages. Their light is transmitted to Earth and we have to become pure channels of cosmic energy for our own healing and purification as well as the Earth's.

We are all part of an eternal divine plan which is not limited to patterns and forms. All creation exists in unity. We all receive and transmit light. We are all creators and we have the tools to maintain balance not only in us but also in all beings that are connected to us. When humanity suffers from imbalances and distortion, the planet is also suffering from the same imbalance. The illusion and fragmentation are the symptoms.

When a planet is not able to receive cosmic light because of blockages, it has slow growth. This affects the balance of many other beings as well as other planets. The light of our creator should shine on Earth, purification and transformation should take place now.

Wisdom of Thoth: The separation within a being

Human beings are taught to experience realities that are based on the mind's calculations and stored information as well as the effect of external distorted forces that can create beliefs, fears, limitations, imbalances, imperfections, stagnation and schisms.

Human beings are convinced that everything that is in the mind should be organized, fully accepted and followed. So people keep thinking, organizing, analyzing, defining, living with their fears and limitations and allowing them to grow. Human beings step into the world of illusion, which also exists in the mind, and start to fantasize, expecting, hoping to receive a reward that does not exist, missing the opportunities offered by the greatness of the present moment and the flow of life.

All this confusion can only lead to separation within a being; it leads people to live their lives without knowing their purpose, their true gifts, their energy and its connection with their physical body, the true power of growth that all beings carry and the light that guides them to experience growth.

You may have been taught to focus on the mind but your true and natural state is to experience your being and dive deep and reach the core of your existence. At the core of your being, you connect to the light of your astral body. If you wish to connect to your astral existence and its powerful growth learn to be in peace away from the mind and deep into the abundance of the being and the eternal light.

119

Introduction

What separates you from your true self? Why can you not see your purpose clearly?

The gods' intention is to awaken the human beings on Earth; show them the way out of the maze of illusion, help them to connect to their true selves and recognize their tools and purpose. All creative forces in the cosmos want to enable humanity to connect to and heal with Earth. All living beings on Earth will support humanity to experience its true purpose and support collective growth on the planet.

The gods want to communicate with all beings on Earth and heal all imbalances and blockages. Their light is transmitted to Earth and we have to become pure channels of cosmic energy for our own healing and purification as well as Earth's.

Wisdom of Thoth: Your creators exist in you

All human beings on Earth carry the light of astral existence. Everything exists in unity in the cosmos. The physical existence and the astral body remain united and share growth, transformation and cosmic communications.

The astral body allowed the opportunity of reincarnation to take place and light from its astral existence travelled to the Earth's space to cocreate with her powerful forces a physical being that carries the light of an astral body.

Humans should experience the cosmic law of unity to support healing, clarity and expansion in their being. This truth is vital and will guide them back to their pure state away from the fantasies and illusions of the mind. Your creators exist in you. They are supporting you in this present moment. They want to show you your path of abundance, and the countless opportunities that the life flow offers to you constantly, endlessly.

Experience the creative forces within you; the light of the cosmos and the divine light that support the astral light in your Earth being and then connect the creative powers of Earth that are constantly creating and nourishing life in her being. Earth was given the power to create, connecting to the light and having countless transformations and phases of growth. If you really want to experience constant joy and fulfillment, connect to your powerful creators and experience the truth about your existence, life on Earth and the creation of the cosmos. Allow truth to open up doors for you that will support connections on Earth and in the cosmos.

Introduction

Dive into the greatness of your being and see how powerful you really are. The power that you are can be seen in the design of your physical body and the aura that are constantly supporting the growth processes in your being. Your power is a cosmic gift and is stored in the core of your being. Connecting to your core, you allow your power to grow within your being. Every part of you is experiencing this cosmic gift; everything that you communicate and create is built on your power to grow with the cosmos.

Focus on your power. Focus on the way your being can achieve balance and maintain life with all your different organs working together, being generated by energies. See yourself as a physical body connected to Earth but also as an extension of your astral body.

When you understand that the astral plane is your home and you will return there at the end of this reincarnation then you will be able to allow the cosmic light to go through you and have a life of balance and growth. When you are able to achieve this, humanity will connect to you energetically in order to receive the same gift. You will become the seed for Earth's transformation and you will bring cosmic light to the planet for healing and rebirth.

Wisdom of Thoth: Dive into the greatness of your being

The astral experience is not separate from the physical experience. Everything that has life exists and grows in unity. Separation and division exist in the mind. Human beings will have to stop focusing on the mind and seek connection with all life starting with their own being.

Dive into the greatness of your being and see how powerful you really are. The power that you are can be seen in the design of your physical body and the aura that is constantly supporting the growth processes in your being. The mind will either ignore the aura or will label it as something separate from you.

The same mental process of division will be used when you try to define your astral existence. You may start asking the following questions: where is it; how far is it from my physical existence; what are the obstacles that restrict me from experiencing my astral body; can I connect to it and what methods should I use; is it important to connect to my astral existence or perhaps it is a door that will remain closed for human beings?

The mind will take you through different diversions to show you that truth does not exist. The light in the core of your being is the connector between the physical and the astral existence and you experience it when you enter the state of peace. Learning to move away from the mind is purification; connecting to your whole being and your understanding of it in your truth. This is not a method but a constant journey that takes you closer to the light and the astral existence.

Introduction

People who are able to follow their purpose, are connecting to their true-self. Many human beings on Earth are not able to achieve that because they accept illusion as truth and live a life with a social purpose. All beings need to start experiencing truth and freedom in their lives because the unity of the two is a driving force that can lead you to your true self and guide you to fulfill your purpose.

Existing in a peaceful state means that you exist in unity with your whole being and you allow the cosmic energy to go through you connecting the astral and the physical body. When you are in a meditative state and you are able to disconnect from all illusion, negativity and artificiality, you exist in a space that is limitless.

You experience constant growth that has nothing to do with challenges and obstacles and it is experienced by you like a flow of immense power of transformation. When you are in this state you connect to the astral plane. You are opening up to unlimited opportunities of cosmic existence and this knowing is transferred to your physical body.

Wisdom of Thoth: Everything exists in unity!

The astral plane exists in you and supports your cosmic existence on Earth. It is a powerful state that is available for you to experience when you disconnect from the mind and free yourself, entering a state of peace.

When you disentangle yourself from illusionary beliefs, fears, expectations and limitations, you are entering a space of peace that allows you to reconnect to your truth and pure state, to your cosmic existence.

Having a physical body and a life on Earth does not stop you from connecting to the cosmos in you and around you. Everything exists in unity! You are always part of the cosmos because your life form is supported by cosmic light.

There is an unbroken connection that ties all life forms together and this is the cosmic and divine light that created them. Human beings were created to connect to the light and its powerful qualities in order to maintain life.

This is a high gift and duty and should be experienced by all beings at all times. Your reality is not your stories, events, choices, decisions, explanations, obstacles or diversions. Your truth is the growth and transformation that is happening in your being in this present moment with the support of the light that is entering your being. Do not block vital processes of growth by remaining in your mind locked in an illusionary reality.

Introduction

You are here to receive the light and heal yourself from the illusion of separation and polarity which has given birth to fear, confusion and survival. There are many human beings on Earth who are longing to achieve clarity, connecting to their true purpose, but they are entangled in the web of illusion and limitation. Thoth wants to nourish all beings with light and teachings: when people are able to empty their minds from illusionary beliefs, aspirations, needs, suffering, pleasures and expectations, they will discover their creator. When humans are able to heal distortion, they will support the planet's growth and transformation. There are many people on Earth who are walking the path of awakening. Their numbers are going to grow; this is the divine plan.

The cosmic light is reaching Earth to help her disconnect from illusion and artificiality; this can happen when everything that exists on the planet opens up to receive the light and transmit it to others. Opening up to cosmic light is a natural process available to all beings in all planes.

If you think that you are not able to connect to the light, it means that illusion, blockages and trauma have locked you in a space of non-clarity, non-truth and non-growth. Being in this space you cannot connect to your true self and purpose; you cannot heal and experience growth but also you cannot offer the gifts of knowing and transformation to others. You can be free when you start observing yourself and go beyond the persona and the ego.

Earth is supporting your growth; open up to receive the healing that will lead you to purification and transformation. When you are able to recognise illusion then your connection to Earth will become stronger. There will be no obstacles in your way and this is how you will be able to create a life of truth, freedom and growth according to your divine plan.

Wisdom of Thoth: An everlasting flow of cosmic abundance

Earth is in constant communication with her astral body. She is a living being that experiences life, has a physical form and energy field and is also closely connected to her astral body that supports her ability to create life.

To become a creator, you have to be a powerful receiver and transmitter of light. The light of the cosmos should enter your being as an everlasting flow of cosmic abundance and bring countless opportunities for growth and transformation that you will freely experience.

To be able to constantly receive the cosmic light and be in constant transformation, you have to accept your cosmic existence and your astral body. The light will guide you to experience cosmic growth and your astral existence, it will show you the energy fields that unite all planes and how the flow of life is supported and maintained.

You will experience the vastness of cosmic creation and you will know that all living beings have the potential of being a creator; creating and supporting life in the cosmos. You cannot remain in ignorance regarding your true path, growth processes but also the collective growth of the planet that is part of a vast cosmic creation and fantasizing about creating greatness in your life. You cannot live in an illusionary reality full of limitations and obstacles when you want to create with truth and purity. Purification is an important step to connecting to the light and becoming a creator.

Introduction

The astral plane is a living being and receives the light in order to transform and grow and its growth cycles and transformations have created a vast astral plane that has countless sub-planes of different vibrations and living beings that exist on these planes.

We are all connected to each other and energy, which is information, passes from one being to another. Your intention should be to connect to your true self and fulfil your purpose. You are always supported when you are growing similar to the seed that is planted in the ground. Your growth processes are known to the light and all living beings that experienced transformation as they enter their pure state of existence.

The cosmic light will flow in and offer you all the nourishment that you need to clear imbalances. You can acquire awareness when you acknowledge the light in us and use it as a guide. When human beings connect to their true self, they will be able to follow their purpose and have a life full of remarkable and liberating experiences.

Wisdom of Thoth: The core of all living beings

Now human beings should know that gods do not have physical bodies and a simple explanation for their existence is that they are light and are created to co-exist with the cosmic light to support and maintain life in all planes.

There was a time that the astral core was transforming in order to become the astral plane. All living beings have a light core in them and in the depths of this core can be found a cosmic seed placed there by the cosmic light and the gods.

The astral plane is a living being and receives the light in order to transform and grow and its growth cycles and transformations have created a vast astral plane that has countless sub-planes of different vibrations and living beings that exist on these planes.

Some of you may ask: why was it necessary for these living beings to be created? The cosmic light created energy fields, energy points, connections and movement that support the unity and growth and the whole astral plane. The astral beings were created as energy points. They were created by the astral plane creator receiving the light of the cosmos and the divine light.

Similarly to Earth, creating living beings to support her growth and expansion, the astral plane formed astral beings and they have been growing over a limitless period of time. It is part of their purpose to be powerful receivers and transmitters of light and support astral growth by experiencing themselves and all astral beings that are connected to them.

When astral beings are powerful receivers and transmitters of light they have fulfilled their purpose in this present time. They are tuned into the greater cycles of growth that are experienced by the astral plane. They are given additional duties, such as spreading the light to lower vibrational sub-planes, reincarnating on physical planes or to guiding astral beings that they have reincarnated. They can also connect to the high light of the gods and support them to create cosmic light.

Introduction

Earth is an organism that follows cosmic laws by design. Her size and position in the galaxy support the planet's link with the sun and allow some expansion. A galaxy does not exist separately from other planetary systems; it is a microcosm within a macrocosm, a receiver and transmitter of light that allows the flow of life.

Galaxies experience growth and this depends on all planets acting as a unified force connecting to the sun and having the ability to receive and transmit cosmic light. It seems that the planets are trying to stay connected to the sun but also the sun's quality to transmit light strengthens this connection with the planets.

The sun receives cosmic light when it is connected to other suns and then transmits it to the planets that form a galaxy around it. This is an important duty; when the sun transmits light to the planets it also teaches them not only to receive it but also to transmit it to everything that connects to them.

Wisdom of Thoth: The core of the Earth

Earth is a powerful creator and has experienced a phase of growth that is known as the golden era where cosmic and divine light was reaching Earth as a constant and uninterrupted flow and supported Earth's ability to create. The cosmic and divine light was able to enter Earth through her astral body.

The core of the Earth is a being that can exist in the physical plane as well as the astral plane. It is a powerful connector between the two planes and a portal that allows cosmic growth to enter the physical body of the planet. You may think that Earth as a physical body is the creator of all the abundance that you can see on the planet.

Earth creates from the core of her being. The astral and physical existence are united to support and develop their creative gifts as she is growing towards her golden era. Earth wants to support living beings on the planet to become creators. The divine and cosmic light should flow through all beings showing them their beautiful gifts and true path and ways to create abundance in their lives as well as supporting collective growth.

All living beings that exist on the planet right now should abandon fears, limitations and confusion and dive into the abundance of Earth and the core of her being where all her powerful creative abilities grow. Earth will support you to become a creator and exist in a state of abundance.

Introduction

Planets are living beings and connect to their astral existence. The core of their being carries great power and a powerful truth that allows planets to become creators. They experience many phases of transformation and growth, connected to the divine and cosmic light. All life that they create is designed to connect to the core of the planet and the light that flows within the planet's being.

All planets are alive. Earth is a unique living being with a unique creation. Life can exist in different forms. Most planets have many resources eternally and they are able to create and nourish different types of beings who exist there. Life is abundant in the universe.

Wisdom of Thoth: Life on other planets

Many of you may have questions about life on other planets. The cosmic and divine light sees the physical plane where all physical life is created as one being. All physical beings are connected and supported by their astral existence.

Planets are living beings and connect to their astral existence and the core of their being to allow them to become creators. They experience many phases of deep and profound metamorphosis, as they connect to the divine and cosmic light. All life that they create is designed to connect to the core of the planet and the light that flows within the planet's being.

When the physical plane was created, all planets were designed to grow together and experience similar processes of growth. This process was interrupted when the planets developed the ability to absorb the light, create life and share their light with other living beings.

There were planets that were not able to grow constantly and effortlessly. Their ability to connect and constantly create life was restricted. Planets and the living beings that were part of their creation were affected by imbalances that created schisms and patterns of limitation.

Certain planets were destroyed and this created a powerful distortion that brought the fear of death and survival. Planets did not support the collective growth of the physical plane, they exist in separation. They go through different processes of growth, their physical forms are not the same and the life that they create has different abilities and opportunities to grow and receive the light. However all planets are creators and when they stop to create, they stop to exist.

Introduction

Planets are living organisms and when they are in alignment they connect energetically and affect each other's cosmic laws and systems. There is unity and we are all part of this alignment able to strengthen the bonds and the energy that flows through it. Our duty as energetic beings is to strengthen and support Earth's alignment with our own light and the clarity of our intention.

You have to use your energy to strengthen bonds on Earth: bonds between people, activities, spirits, energy fields, actions, thoughts and imperfections. Accept it all and then embrace it all. Also teach others to do the same, physically or energetically so we can all travel together and expand. This is a new era that will be embraced and celebrated by all.

Wisdom of Thoth: Creator planets

All planets are creators and being supported by the cosmic and divine light, they are creating life. Planets do not carry the same light and do not have the same abilities to grow and create. There are different natural laws on each planet that reflect the cosmic laws in various ways.

Planets create different physical forms that have their own unique ways to grow and transform. The planets support the growth of the living beings that they create but this depends on their own ability to connect to their astral body, receive and transmit light and expand toward the cosmos.

Earth is able to create life on the surface as well as the inner parts. For Earth to grow, all the parts need to connect, communicate, share energies and support collective growth and transformation. Other planets' life forms exist mainly in the inner parts and are tuned into the collective growth and the connection to the cosmic and divine light.

Living beings in a pure state want to connect to the core of the planet that created their physical body because it is the most powerful part and carries the greatest light. Powerful physical beings that experience the cosmos in their body and energy create unique civilizations that are devoid of distortion and illusion. These beings and their creator planet support the light to travel through the cosmos, enter the physical plane and reach all living beings on all planets.

Introduction

The physical plane consists of countless planets and astral systems and they all created unique elements and natural laws. Many living beings cannot exist on other planets because the elements, energies and support they receive from the core of the planet are different. Most living beings do not want to travel to other planets, instead, they want to remain grounded, stay open to all the nourishment and support they can receive and grow to experience their unique body, gifts, path and purpose.

Wisdom of Thoth: Travelling to other planets

Planets within a galaxy or star system can have a different physical appearance: size, shape, elements, rotation or position in relation to other planets and the sun. Therefore, the physicality that is created by each planet is quite unique.

Many living beings cannot exist on other planets because the elements, energies and support they receive from the core of the planet are different. Most living beings do not want to travel to other planets, instead, they want to remain grounded, stay open to all the nourishment and support they can receive and grow, experiencing their unique body, gifts, path and purpose.

Living beings who wish to travel to other planets have as a motif the search for new resources and colonization as well as escaping a physical disaster or the destruction of a planet. Communication between living beings that exist on different planets can be achieved energetically and through the cosmic and divine flow that unites all life.

The physical plane can be seen as a space of diversity and plurality where planets and their creation have unique gifts and purpose, and can develop communities, civilizations and connections that can help them grow or distract them from growth. All living beings on all planets should purify and support the planet's collective growth. The purpose of living beings on the physical plane is to bring light to the planet and support collective transformation and expansion. This will enable the planets to receive light and create powerful energy fields for the light to reach all beings constantly.

Introduction

Illusion is easily accepted by human beings that follow mechanical patterns. They remain passive and are open to being spoon-fed any false reality. They enjoy when they have to do nothing; they are presented with many choices and opportunities which are all illusionary. Humans are an easy target for those who create illusions; they are the type of consumers who will buy everything at any price. There is a reason for that: it is their trauma and the fear of survival that have taken away the clarity.

When physical beings simplify the way they experience their being and life on the planet, eliminate restrictions, unnatural expectations, distortion, artificiality, patterns, illusionary beliefs, the fear of survival and separation, they will be free to experience their true path and purpose.

This will help them grow collectively in a pure state. Distorted communities often form a pyramid and at the top, there is a small group of people whose only focus is to maintain and strengthen the influence of the pyramid in the mind of a living being.

Wisdom of Thoth: Simplicity supports growth

Planets can maintain their unique characteristics and still become powerful creators, receivers and transmitters of cosmic light. When physical beings simplify the way they experience their being and life on the planet, eliminate restrictions, unnatural expectations, distortion, artificiality, patterns, illusionary beliefs, the fear of survival and separation, they will be free to experience their true path and purpose.

This will help them grow collectively in a pure state. Distorted communities often form a pyramid and at the top, there is a small group of people whose only focus is to maintain and strengthen the influence of the pyramid in the mind of a living being.

All thoughts and beliefs of people should reflect the existence of the pyramid structure. All systems, mechanisms, communication and satisfaction are affected by the desperate need for the pyramid to exist and rule. When living beings are restricted to experience a limited and distorted life, they have to remember that they were created to be creators for the planet.

You can be a creator when you are free from limitations and open to experiencing planetary and cosmic growth. The state of restrictions is a small artificial state that does not allow growth. You have the power to exit the pyramid perception and enter the state of cosmic abundance where everything grows as one.

Introduction

The cosmic light brings life to the whole cosmic creation. When the cosmic light enters your being, every part of you is united with the core and all schisms are healed. Your physical body, energy and light are receiving cosmic guidance that helps them to grow while they are experiencing unity. When you connect to the cosmic light, you connect to everything that exists. You are in communication with our Source and this communication can transform you, heal you and support your growth.

When the light enters your being, brings balance and unity to your whole existence and it also brings clarity, knowing and connection to your true self, the Earth and the cosmos. Human beings are created to be Earth's receivers and transmitters of light. This way the cosmic light will enter Earth and offer her healing and support all growth processes.

When human beings are suffering from imbalances, they are still able to connect to the cosmic light but imbalances act as a blockage and restrict healing and purification.

Having a pure intention to connect to your true self, the cosmic light will guide you and help you to purify your whole being. This experience will bring you transformation because you are opening up to the light and you are co-creating a new balanced existence of you. If you do not have a pure intention and you are not focusing on truth then imbalances will remain and in most cases they will expand and grow.

Wisdom of Thoth: Illusionary realities

There are many planets that are not able to purify themselves from different forms of distortion and this may create schisms and many diversions regarding the unity and collective growth of the planet.

Living beings can turn against the natural laws, their true purpose and path and disconnect from the cosmic abundance that exists in them and around them. Living beings tend to create communities that are disconnected from the light in the core and the power of creation. Instead, they allow distortion to create illusionary realities whose core power is the social pyramid control.

The pyramid living structure does not follow natural or cosmic laws and influences living beings to disconnect from their being and its natural process of transformation and growth. The natural laws of a planet are a reflection of the cosmic laws and when living beings experience them, they are in a pure state connecting to the astral existence, allowing the divine and cosmic light to enter their being.

The light will always guide them to their path and the purpose of their current lifetime. It will guide them inwards towards the core of their being and will teach them that they can grow in unity with all life. Schisms, separation, poralities and fragmentation are diversions separating you from the truth that you are. If your communities allow these forms of separation, you exist in a distorted pyramid structure illusion.

Introduction

All beings that reincarnate on Earth are responsible for connecting to the light in them; helping their vibration to rise and the trauma to be healed. Human beings have many opportunities in their lifetime to grow.

When you understand the importance of reaching to the core of your being and experiencing your light, you will allow it to transform you.

When you are tuning into the light, you are connecting to the cosmos. This discovery will lead you to a new metamorphosis and then your path is open and your purpose will be clear to you. The vision of the high creator gods is that the people wake up to their true potential and assist Earth with her own awakening.

Wisdom of Thoth: The journey of growth

The light of the cosmos has the power to unite all life in all planes and connect it to the powerful organism, the astral plane which was created by the intention of the source. All living beings in the physical plane, connect to the astral plane by focusing on the core of the being that carries great light and expand to experience collective growth.

Astral light exists in the core of all physical beings. All parts are connected and turned into this eternal creative power that co-created with Earth your physical existence. In order to understand and fully experience life on Earth, human beings have to experience the light in them. When this happens all powerful connections in humans come alive and the light flows through every part of you and brings growth. You will be guided on your path.

Your understanding and experience of your path and purpose, it is not the final destination. Your final destination is a state of expansion towards the core of the planet reaching collective growth and astral existence.

Everything that you are, share, receive or create should focus on this journey of growth. When living beings have grown to achieve this, their connection to other living beings and the planet becomes powerful, their life reflects their purpose and their transition from the physical to the astral existence is an effortless flow of transformation. Living beings on all planets and planes experience unity within their being and as they remain open to continue their journey of growth, they expand towards the core of all creation, the astral core that is in constant connection to the intention of the source.

Introduction

Your being is a microcosm of the vast, eternal and powerful astral plane. Your being follows the cosmic laws of unity, constant growth and transformation. It exists to experience the flow of life moving within and attracting the cosmic and divine light to constantly create in it. All our special tools and talents are stored in the body and are waiting for us to discover them. When you know your body, you understand that it is a microcosm of high creation and a link to all life. Your body is your temple and path for growth and expansion to other realms.

Do not miss the opportunity to experience life using your physical body; however, you do not need to diversify from your true purpose, getting lost in the five-sense reality. If you are not wise you can find yourself in a five-sense labyrinth with no way out. I hope that you follow this guidance and create the balance needed between all bodies and all their expressions.

If you were able to see beyond Earth and galaxy formations, you could understand that the physical body is a microcosm of the cosmos. There are countless galaxies joined together, affecting each other's growth; their movement is synchronized similarly to the movement in your own body.

Wisdom of Thoth: Life is a precious gift

Light beings that reincarnate on the physical plane have an important duty: to support planetary growth by building bridges between the physical plane and the astral. For this to happen they have to strengthen many connections, starting with communication with their own being.

Your being is a microcosm of the vast, eternal and powerful astral plane. Your being follows the cosmic laws of unity, constant growth and transformation. It exists to experience the flow of life moving within and attracting the cosmic and divine light to constantly create in it.

Life for all beings is a precious gift, a state of power, joy and abundance. All the gifts that you receive when the cosmic light enters your being and supports you on your path, have to be transmitted to others. This is how life is maintained and growth opportunities can be created for all beings.

When beings create using their unique gifts, they create bridges for the light of the cosmos to enter the physical plane, spread to all living beings and reach the core of the planet. The planet that is a receiver of light will also become a transmitter. It will build bridges for the light to travel to other planets and purify the whole physical plane.

The cosmic and divine light has created this plane and their duty is to nourish it and support its growth following the cosmic laws. They are planets and star systems that are more powerful receivers and transmitters than others. They are going through high growth and creating bridges to help the light travel in their being and spread to the whole physical plane.

Introduction

Signs of the golden age are still apparent in the inner parts of the planet and affect their growth. All beings who exist there are able to connect to high energies; this allows Earth to continue being a creator.

Many of you have reincarnated on Earth in order to connect to her energies and allow the cosmic light to heal the schisms. The human beings that are reincarnating on Earth right now are brought to create a bridge between the planet and the Source.

The bridge will be cemented by the cosmic light that is the extension of the Source and brings life to all beings in the cosmos. Unity brings life to all. This is why all parts of Earth need to be united and exchange energies of healing and purification; all beings should unite in order to start Earth's purification and transformation.

The inner Earth is divided into different layers and there are more resources and space for civilizations to grow and flourish. These civilizations are not competitive with each other because they recognize that they are all Earth's creation. They experience the cosmic laws of unity and growth and they create with the light. The powerful energies of the Earth's core are spreading and nourishing all life in the inner parts of the Earth.

Wisdom of Thoth: The inner parts of the Earth

In the physical plane can be found various forms of distortion, imbalances, schisms and impurities that affect the growth of living beings. There are planets that understand the cosmic laws and they focus on purifying from these impurities and all life forms united experience a state of high growth. They become the powerful light bringers, the great architects that will unite the physical and the astral plane.

Earth is experiencing the golden era in her core and inner parts. There is a strong bond between the physical and the astral body of Earth. There are bridges connecting the core and the astral body, allowing the light to enter and support Earth's powerful creative abilities.

The bridges expand to the inner parts of the planet where living beings have created civilizations of light and truth and have accepted that their path and purpose of their lifetime is to carry and share the divine and cosmic light. They exist in unity with Earth and support her growth. Earth is experiencing her golden era in the inner parts of her being and all her creation has a life of abundance, inner joy and high creativity.

The inner Earth is divided into different layers and there are more resources and space for civilizations to grow and flourish. These civilizations are not competitive with each other because they recognize that they are all Earth's creation. They experience the cosmic laws of unity and growth and they create with the light. The powerful energies of the Earth's core are spreading and nourishing all life in the inner parts of the planet.

Introduction

The light that exists in Earth's core needs to travel to her whole being and bring balance to everything that exists on the planet. Humanity is looking for its purpose, looking for the creative force that can clear distortion and can bring healing and growth. It is important that humans become a true channel for this light and support it to spread through the planet.

Your purpose in this lifetime is linked to the purpose of the planet and it is your responsibility to bring this light up to the surface. Exist in unity with people that understand this important task and together you can purify yourselves and create bridges between Earth's high growth and her schisms. Humanity needs healing in order to connect to its true self. This healing can be shared and become the root of the Golden era to be activated and reach the whole planet. When this happens enlightenment will affect the whole planet and show that illusion does not exist.

Wisdom of Thoth: Life in the inner parts of the Earth

You may want to know more about life in the inner parts of the Earth. You may have questions such as: What type of resources can be found in the inner parts and what type of civilizations were created there; why beings from the surface of the Earth cannot enter the inner parts and coexist with the living there?

When Earth creates, she receives the cosmic and divine light in the core of her being. The core is a combination of astral and physical existence. It is a bridge that unites the astral and the physical as well as being a powerful point of transformation on Earth's body.

Earth's powerful energies will connect to the cosmic light in the core and this is how creation starts to happen. Earth's elements that are used to create physical existence are created in the core and spread to the whole planet creating life forms. Earth offers abundance to all living beings that grow on the planet and wants life to be maintained and transformed according to natural and cosmic laws.

The living beings that exist in the inner parts are able to see and experience abundance in the present moment. These beings do not doubt, question or ignore the abundance that is created by Earth, instead, they allow it to shape their reality, living on the planet. There are beings on the surface of the Earth that experience abundance and effortless growth.

These beings exist in unity with the planet and all her creation and they support uninterrupted growth on a personal and collective level. They are the ones who bring light to the surface of the Earth and want to heal beings who exist in a confused and distorted state.

Introduction

Distortion and illusion do not exist in the inner parts. The communities and civilizations that exist there do not compete with each other and do not wish to colonize or become an authority. They exist in Earth's abundance and focus on the planet's growth and how they can support it.

If you were able to enter the core of the Earth you would realise that it is much more active and has a much higher vibration than the surface of the planet and offers high growth to all parts of the planet including the surface. The same is happening with the astral plane. It is a non-physical life form of high vibration and growth that feeds all creation.

There is a wave of high energies coming from the core of the Earth, reaching the surface and moving into her aura. Earth is experiencing regeneration and rebirth in areas around her core and this is projected to all expressions of life that can be found in these parts of the planet. We are able to exchange cosmic energy and offer healing and awakening to the planet. These energies are also going to affect life on the surface of the planet. The ones who are awake will be supported in their quest for truth and detachment from illusion.

Wisdom of Thoth: The beings in the inner parts of the Earth

The beings in the inner parts of the Earth have different physical forms that do not resemble the human form. They have a longer life cycle and use their energy to communicate, create and share with others.

Their civilization is not based on the pyramid structure that can be seen on the surface of the Earth and they do not experience restrictions and limitations. The beings in the inner parts are free to live with Earth and experience the abundance that she is creating for them. They are aware that their purpose is to receive the light through her body as well as build bridges between Earth and the cosmos.

Distortion and illusion do not exist in the inner parts. The communities and civilizations that exist there do not compete with each other and do not wish to colonize or become an authority. They exist in Earth's abundance and focus on the planet's growth and how they can support it. Some of you may ask: Do they want to communicate and co-exist with humans on the surface of the planet? They are not curious about life on Earth.

They are able to communicate with all life energetically, they share light and growth with all living beings on the planet. They follow Earth's pure intention which is to share abundance with all and support collective growth. Human beings on the surface of the Earth can connect to all life energetically and support the collective growth of the planet. Distortions, imbalances and limitations can evaporate from all parts of the Earth when all living beings unite and have a common purpose: the collective growth and the task of building bridges between the cosmos and Earth.

Introduction

The creation that exists in the inner parts of the planet is Earth's divinity. You exist on the surface and this is what you know as the planet Earth.

On the surface there is a web of illusion that affects all living beings, their growth and consciousness. But there is a strong need for awakening brought to humanity by the helpers of the Gods who have reincarnated on Earth to bring the light of the Cosmos on Earth.

There were many beings on Earth who were instructed by the Gods and the light of the cosmos to experience a life cycle on Earth and try to raise people's consciousness. Some of them created mystery schools and sacred communities and others were the advisers of great rulers.

We are instructed once again to bring light to Earth because the planet is in a process of evolution. This will affect not only Earth and her creation but the whole cosmos. You are witnessing our attempt to communicate with planet Earth and we want you to be part of this communication by becoming true receivers and transmitters of our energy and the cosmic light.

So how can you achieve that and why is it important? The whole of humanity can become the bridge for our light to go through and reach Earth. You are an energetic map that can lead us to the Earth's schism and allow us to heal her. Your reward will be freedom from all limitations and negativity and the rising of a new consciousness.

If you want to become the bridge between the cosmos and the planet, you need to have pure intention. You are the toddler that wants to walk; you are the leaf that bursts out from the wooden branch; you are the sun ray that brings life to Earth; you are the rain that nourishes all creation. There is so much purity on Earth; there is life and growth that has not been affected by fragmentation and illusion because it follows the cosmic laws. This is what you have to do too. Look around you for purity, tune in to it and then discover your own purity. This will be the beginning of your path.

Wisdom of Thoth: Collective Purification

Earth is going through a powerful process of purification and its purpose is for Earth to regain balance, eliminate physical and energetic imbalances and allow all her creation to experience collective growth. Many bridges are being built right now to support connection and communication between Earth and her creation. There is no true separation between Earth and all living beings that exist and grow on the planet.

Separation is an illusionary state created by distortion in the mind of human beings. This division not only creates schisms between Earth and living beings but also supports imbalances within the being. Humans often complain about their inability to communicate, love and heal their body, their fear of survival, lack and self-worth. They experience negative emotions and struggle to move along when there are so many obstacles. They have problems with relationships; they feel betrayed, abandoned and isolated. They worry about finances, rewards, expectations and career opportunities.

All these experiences support schisms and imbalances within the being and reflect humans' illusionary belief that they exist separate from Earth. It seems that the life of a human being is based on an illusion and they close their eyes to the abundance, growth, transformation, unity that exists on Earth.

Human beings can have an effortless life of joy and abundance, connecting and supporting all life on the planet by receiving and transmitting light and being part of the collective growth. Human beings can experience purification with Earth and tune into her energies, the physical body and core. This will clear all illusion and distortion. Problems, imbalances, obstacles, limitations and fears will also disappear. Clarity will be restored and humanity will start to create with Earth.

Introduction

Our light is connected to higher light and when we connect to it, we receive guidance in relation to our purpose and our great gifts. Our spiritual quest is a path that cannot be taught or dictated by other humans because they are on their own unique paths and their understanding is formed by their own unique purpose. Our true purpose is bare of feelings and logic. It is our inheritance from the astral plane where we exist in a pure form.

There are parts of our being that can show us the way to empowerment and our achievement is always linked with somebody else's growth. The hands of a healer know the healer's journey and as he/she empowers others with healing, the healer receives light, clarity and greater abilities. When you are a pure channel of the gods' light, you are going to connect to people who can help you with your transformation and you give this great gift back to them.

For life to be maintained, all living beings have to fully experience unity. Living beings are energy points in a field that has to grow and expand. The energy points grow with the field when they receive and transmit light to each other. They accept unity because it is the power that supports growth. Energy points do not see themselves as an isolated unit but they are the creators of the field, they exist in unity with it.

Wisdom of Thoth: Unity on Earth

The powerful purification process that Earth is experiencing right now is a long cycle of transformation and will create many opportunities for all life to experience unity and be supported to complete their own growth processes.

It is very important that Earth unites all living beings with the core and have access to powerful energies that carry the light and create abundance on the planet. All living beings have to experience Earth's powerful creative forces growing in the core and supported by Earth's astral body.

For life to be maintained, all living beings have to fully experience unity. Living beings are energy points in a field that has to grow and expand. The energy points grow with the field when they receive and transmit light to each other. They accept unity because it is the power that supports growth. Energy points do not see themselves as an isolated unit but they are the creators of the field, they exist in unity with it.

All energy points are tuned to the light flow and become creators with the light. Unity should be restored on Earth and all living beings can share the greatness and abundance that she is creating and stay open to receive countless opportunities for growth.

Human beings have to heal the schisms within to be able to connect to their true path and experience abundance and effortless life. Their own purification brings them closer to the core of the Earth and the collective growth. When all beings unite to the core of the Earth, they will experience the power of the astral plane in her body and then they will know that growth possibilities are endless for all beings.

Introduction

Illusion can take many forms and can capture the people that are looking for truth. To avoid this and truly disconnect from all artificiality you have to look in you, your connection with your astral body and the Earth's energies.

Connecting to truth will help you understand your true purpose and how to connect to cosmic growth and high light. When you achieve clarity, you will connect to your true self and you will follow a process of transformation, growth and wellbeing.

Light from the astral plane has to flow to all living beings and support their growth and their ability to receive and transmit light. For this to happen all living beings have to experience unity with their true self and path, body and energy as well as the light in them.

Wisdom of Thoth: The great plan of purification

The physical plane with all its planets, astral systems, galaxies and living beings has to exist in unity with the astral plane. Light from the astral plane has to flow to all living beings and support their growth and their ability to receive and transmit light. For this to happen all living beings have to experience unity with their true self and path, body and energy as well as the light in them.

Living beings will have to purify themselves in order to create bridges of communication with their whole being, become aware of all growth processes and remove illusionary realities that are veils of deception. Peace, self-love, clarity, regeneration, transformation and growth should be the ground that experiences growth.

When living beings are purified they can observe the greater plan of purification that transforms the lives of all living beings on Earth. Purification when experienced collectively brings unity to Earth.

All beings tune to the core of the planet and start receiving powerful light that allows them to understand cosmic unity. When you grow with Earth, you will continue to expand towards the astral plane and create more bridges between the birthplace of all life that was created by the intention of the source, and life that grows this present moment in the physical plane. When everything grows as one, limitations, distortion, illusions and imbalances stop existing. All living beings are free to experience life as an effortless flow that always moves towards one direction, the source.

CHAPTER VIII

Beings that exist close to the Source were given the task to maintain life and create life through the cosmic light. In the cosmos, there is no superiority or inferiority; the low and high position of influence; possessions and power over other beings; ambitions, deceit, illusionary success and failure. In the cosmos there are no divisions; we all experience unity and our task are related to our essence and growth.

Introduction

All living beings exist in unity with the vast creation of our source. The physical body connects you to the Earth's energies and shows you how to create with the resources that exist on the planet. Your five senses are also messengers of information and humans on Earth have almost exhausted all different ways of experiencing life with their senses.

Existing in a peaceful state means that you exist in unity with your whole being and you allow the cosmic energy to go through you connecting the astral and the physical body. When you are in a meditative state and you are able to disconnect from all illusion, negativity and artificiality, you exist in a space that is limitless.

You experience constant growth that has nothing to do with challenges and obstacles and it is experienced by you like a flow of immense power of transformation. When you are in this state you connect to the astral plane. You are opening up to unlimited opportunities of cosmic existence and this knowing is transferred to your physical body.

When you are able to achieve this, your imbalances will be diminished and the illusion will not be strong enough to affect you. Knowing and practising truth, freedom and unity between your astral and physical body, will transform you into a high receiver and transmitter of light. You will be able then to achieve your purpose and transform humanity and Earth.

Wisdom of Thoth: Inner communication

The light in the core of your being is the path that you have to take to help you connect to the astral plane. All planes coexist and support each other's growth. The astral plane is the core of the cosmos and when it is experiencing growth and transformation, all planes and sub-planes should connect and and grow with it.

The light that is responsible for growth, will transfer the transformation of the astral plane to all planes and create opportunities for them to grow according to the intention of the source. Therefore all living beings need to be in constant communication with the core of their being and experience their light as a door to high states as they are experienced by the astral body.

Some of you may ask: how can human beings achieve this? Humanity is surrounded and controlled by multi-layered manipulation mechanisms that use illusion and distortion to confuse human beings and make them accept illusionary realities as truth.

They focus on beliefs and thoughts that are not the outcome of an experience. They ignore their true being and its purpose of existence, therefore they remain disconnected from the power within. If you are able to purify and untie yourself from all forms of illusion and distortion, your path to know your true self will be open.

You will experience your powerful body that can carry immense transformations, your energy that is constantly expanding and the light that can connect you with the growth of your astral body. All life exists in unity and balance. Your being is created to experience this.

Introduction

Remember that the human state that you are experiencing right now is not permanent; you are astral beings who are in constant evolution and will never be controlled by anything and anybody other than cosmic laws. When human beings are fully awake then they will connect to their true purpose and will allow the high energies to heal Earth. All creation is united to a common goal and this will bring awakening to planet Earth.

Wisdom of Thoth: Connecting to the light in the core of your being

It is time now to dive into your being and connect to the light in the core of your existence. Remain connected to the light and see yourself expanding through the physical body, your energy field and beyond all connections that bring unity to your being.

In this powerful exploration, you will experience that the astral element exists in all planes and in all living beings. It coexists with the elements of the physical body and energy field and it is the one that brings growth and transformation.

Without the astral element, beings will not be able to grow and connect to the cosmic light and the intention of the source. They will not have the opportunity to experience the cosmic laws and the abundance of opportunities that life creates.

The astral element is a powerful light that surrounds all beings and becoming aware of it is a step toward your purpose. Tune into your being and direct your focus on the core. Connect to the light in you that carries the astral element. Ground yourself into this light and experience a unique flow moving through your whole being.

Every part of you is recognizing and tuning into the astral element. You experience expansion, leading you to a new state. Deeper into the essence of life that is created in the astral plane by powerful cosmic forces. You are now expanding towards high creation, your birthplace, a plane that is nourished by the intention of the source in order to grow in its perfection.

Introduction

The astral plane is divided into different sub-planes and this has to do with the type of growth and purpose of the beings that occupy it. At the same time, all sub-planes are connected by cosmic laws and by the light of creation. Your astral body is not solid but it is an energy form that cannot be described by your five senses.

This energy form is in constant transformation and experiences everlasting growth. For this to happen, the astral body needs to connect to the cosmic light. Your astral growth affects your physical experience and growth processes on Earth. If you are able to connect to your true self, fulfil your purpose and support the transformation experienced by Earth and humanity then you have achieved high growth.

Wisdom of Thoth: Experiencing unity

By connecting to the astral element in your being, you not only nourish yourself with high growth and receive cosmic guidance, but you also accept the opportunity to connect to the cosmos.

Having a physical body does not limit you from having this experience; you can tune your whole being into the astral element and experience the immense expansion, connecting your Earth being with the astral body and growth. There are people on Earth who are wondering about parallel lives happening simultaneously in different universes.

To be able to understand this, you have to look at your physical body. Every organ is a "universe" that has its unique life purpose and special abilities to help fulfil its purpose. All organs experience the life flow in their own unique way but they are not isolated. They are aware of other organs; they communicate with them and support each other's growth.

All organs are aware of the collective growth and this is what they seek, trying to fulfil their purpose as life bringers. A similar connection is experienced by all parts of a being. The physical, energetic and astral elements of a being has unique gifts and attract the abundance and perfection of the cosmos in their special way.

They are all states that grow and expand, offering more opportunities to the being to reach the light of the source. In these states, a being can have profound experiences that can transform its whole existence. When you become aware of the different states, the expansion, the opportunities for growth and the experiences in these states then you will understand that life in parallel universes is just your experience of cosmic unity.

Introduction

The seed of all living beings exists in the astral plane. Their astral existence is their permanent experience of high growth that constantly unites them with the source. Living beings will always live, grow and transform even if their life cycle on Earth has ended and their body and energy do not grow anymore.

When humanity wakes up and connects to the cosmos, becoming a transmitter and receiver of light, Earth will experience her connection to the Source and will follow the path of truth, leading to her purpose. When this happens all lower energies that are creating a low-frequency matrix on Earth will have to be banished and all human beings who are supporting this will either purify and grow with Earth or leave the planet.

149

A high-vibrational planet cannot sustain fragmentation, distortion and destruction.

Wisdom of Thoth: Astral existence is their permanent experience of high growth

Some of you may ask: Is it possible for all human beings to experience a connection with their astral body and if it is true why this connection is not effortless? Human beings are living beings that are able to grow and transform on Earth receiving the high light and the powerful energies of the planet. Because of these unique characteristics, we can accept that humans are living beings that experience physicality, energy and the astral element and can effortlessly expand towards these states.

The seed of all living beings' creation exists in the astral plane. Their astral existence is their permanent experience of high growth that constantly unites them with the source. Living beings will always live, grow and transform even if their life cycle on Earth has ended and their body and energy do not grow anymore.

Human beings who focus on the mind, disconnect from their truth and this causes confusion. Due to their confusion and temporary separation from their being, they cannot accept the astral element in them. They often say: I do not know my purpose on Earth; what are my special gifts; I do not know what makes me happy; I cannot find peace; I am struggling with life and I have no support. All these statements create beliefs that show the confusion and isolation of human beings, experiencing illusionary realities controlled by fear and limitation.

Many human beings experience this unnatural state which closes the doors for them to enter cosmic abundance and constant growth. When they are locked into these low vibrational realities they are not able to experience their true existence. This is why connecting to the astral body and expanding towards cosmic growth is a path full of obstacles and diversions. When human beings remove all false, artificial and deceiving life patterns, they will enter a pure state and will effortlessly connect to the astral plane.

Introduction

When humanity suffers from imbalances and distortion, the planet is also suffering from the same imbalance. When a planet is not able to receive cosmic light because of blockages, it has a slow growth. This affects the balance of many other beings as well as other planets. The light of our creator should shine on Earth, purification and transformation should take place now.

We have to unite and connect to the light of our source which is the life-giver. We all have to work against the illusion that has taken over the planet and our weapon is truth. Truth can create miraculous bonds and everything can fall into the right place.

When human beings connect to the truth, they will be able to see their purpose. You will connect to your true self by observing your life patterns and understanding the different ways illusion affects your life.

When people unite and are able to realise that growth is an experience and not a doctrine, not a distant goal that only a few have experienced, growth can be part of your everyday life. When you disconnect from all artificiality and be your true self, you are transforming humanity and Earth.

Wisdom of Thoth: The pathway between Earth and the astral plane

Connecting to your astral body is effortless because you were created to carry the astral element in your being while you are having a reincarnation on Earth. As your light has moved from the astral plane to enter the Earth being and then at the end of a life cycle travels back to the astral plane to reunite with the astral body, the pathway between Earth and the astral plane is always open.

Beings have the opportunity to connect constantly as they receive cosmic light. The cosmic law of unity supports these powerful connections for growth and transformation. There are living beings on Earth that are constantly experiencing communication with their astral body.

The growth and transformation processes that are experienced in the astral plane can be transferred to an Earth being and create powerful opportunities for fulfilled and effortless life on Earth. Growth opportunities are created by the powerful connections between living beings, planes of high growth and cosmic light. When human beings become aware that they exist in an abundance of resources that can help them grow, they will be able to purify from fear patterns, imbalances and limitations. They will return to their pure state and experience a constant connection with the cosmos.

CHAPTER IX

The divine plan is your guide, your true self is the path and the purpose is your destination. Fear has no place in you because it will only take you on a diversion toward limitation. If you allow fear to be your guide then you will experience suffering and disease will start affecting your body. Enter a space of peace and truth will be restored.

Introduction

The next teaching explains the connection between Earth, the astral body and the higher self. Everything that exists is light and energy and is constantly moving within the being, within the aura of a being, connecting to other beings, planets, planes and the cosmos. This is how we describe life, a constant flow of energy. Energy is moving in a circular motion and there is a certain pattern that is followed in order to maintain life and growth. When energies are moving in one's body are clearing, purifying old blockages and imbalances and rejuvenating the body. As energy flows from one being to another, it enables communication and connection and with this, you exchange energy which is very important for your growth.

Wisdom of Thoth: Astral beings, powerful receivers and transmitters

Many human beings are wondering about the connection between the Earth's being, the astral body and the higher self. Are the astral body and the higher self part of the same existence? Does the higher self carry more light or have a unique purpose? Can human beings connect to the higher self and how can they achieve this?

Astral beings have grown into powerful receivers and transmitters of light and were involved in the creation process of the cosmos, supporting the cosmic and divine light to create. Light beings were involved in the creation of fields, and planes and they even experienced reincarnation in order to build bridges between the physical plane and the cosmos.

All the great growth that was experienced by light beings brought a new purpose. For light beings to be able to experience their purpose and increase their ability to grow, they receive high support and guidance. The higher self is part of the light being and its role is to guide and support it in order to fulfil its purpose.

Humans on Earth are supported by their guides and the light in them to experience their path and fulfil their purpose; the higher self offers support and guidance to light beings to experience constant growth and support cosmic creation.

Introduction

The energy in you creates channels of communication; you can visualize them as tunnels of light, similar to star gates that exist in different locations on planet Earth. If people on Earth want to experience accelerated growth and fulfil their purpose, they have to allow their energy to connect them to many energetic fields not only on Earth but also in the astral plane. The cosmic and divine light moves through the whole being of the astral existence and when it reaches the higher self it brings guidance about all aspects of the astral being's life: transformation and growth processes that need to happen in order for the cosmic being to fulfil its purpose and support cosmic creation.

Wisdom of Thoth: The higher self of the astral being

The higher self is part of the astral being and offers guidance to help the astral being grow, transform and fulfil its purpose. The cosmic and divine light moves through the whole astral existence and when it reaches the higher self it brings guidance about all aspects of the astral being's life: transformation and growth processes that need to happen in order for the cosmic being to fulfil its purpose and support cosmic creation.

The astral plane is a vast organism and there are countless growth processes happening constantly. The light beings are supporting these processes and they need a compass to be able to navigate and offer the right exchange as it is required from them. Astral beings are supporting energy fields to grow and they also support the connection between all sub-planes with the astral plane.

Their existence focuses on their own growth, the expansion of the astral plane and its connection with all other planes as well as supporting the cosmic and divine light to create new life. Light beings will need some guidance to achieve all these important duties and this guidance can be given by the higher self.

As human beings experience an abundance of support from Earth and the cosmos to help them focus on their path, light beings are also supported by having a direct connection with the light and co-creating with it as well as the higher self that guides the light being to fulfil its purpose.

Introduction

The next teaching answers the following question: can human beings that are having an experience on Earth can also experience the higher self and what will be the benefit of this connection?

When human beings experience their astral body, they receive light that can help them clear blocks and move forward on their path. We all want to connect to the light of the cosmos and the light of our source. This is our purpose, to connect to this high light and transform. It is a very important cosmic law and affects every single being in all planes. You should be able to understand and recognise that your purpose is to connect to the cosmic light. You should live your life to fulfil this purpose. You should connect to others to help them fulfil their purpose.

Wisdom of Thoth: Human beings experiencing the higher self

Some of you may ask: can human beings that are having an experience on Earth, experience the higher self and what will be the benefit of this connection? Human beings have the ability to experience their astral body and its growth and perhaps some of the guidance of the higher self can reach their energy field if it is relevant to their growth processes.

When human beings experience their astral body, they receive light that can help them clear blocks and move forward on their path. All living beings in all planes when they connect to the light or astral growth, receive guidance, healing, expansion and transformation that is related to their purpose and path. Due to distortion on Earth, human beings find it very hard to escape the patterns of distortion which are created by beliefs, dogma and other types of mind manipulation.

A lot of support is available to them by the Earth and the cosmos and all living beings who grow with them. The purpose of the higher self is not to support human life but humans have access to guidance that comes from their astral body and this is supporting them to fulfil their purpose on Earth. The higher self is aware of the divine plan that is created to support reincarnation and guide light beings to experience the transformations of reincarnation. This allows a connection between a human, an astral being and a higher self and offers an exchange of light that brings guidance and support.

Introduction

We all want to connect to the light of the cosmos and the light of our source. This is our purpose, to connect to this high light and transform. This is a very important cosmic law and affects every single being in all planes. You should be able to understand and recognise that your purpose is to connect to the cosmic light. You should live your life to fulfil this purpose. You should connect to others to help them fulfil their purpose. A cosmic truth; it is perfect without limitation, fragmentation and distortion.

Wisdom of Thoth: All living beings receive light

All living beings are connected to energy fields and they are receiving and transmitting light constantly. This way the light moves through the lower planes and creates bonds and connections with the astral plane. Cosmic creation should remain united with the astral plane. If existence in the lower planes can experience a golden era then all distortions, schisms and impurities could be healed and powerful transformations and growth processes can happen.

Unity with the astral plane is the key to growth. Human beings on Earth should connect to their astral existence in order to develop their powerful gift of being a receiver and transmitter of light. Earth provides nourishment, high energies and abundance for growth but she is also a receiver of the light that is coming into a living being. All living beings receive light and create bridges between Earth and the cosmos. With their divine design, they support the unity between the lower planes and the astral plane and allow the golden era to take place.

Introduction

Every living being, including the planets and the universes, is surrounded by an energy field. Your field contains energies that support your Earth's existence and allows you to connect to other energy fields. All beings that are connected to you receive and transmit energies to your field, support the connection and spread the light. These electromagnetic fields are used as receivers and transmitters of energy as well as balancing and regulating the inner and outer light.

Wisdom of Thoth: The creation of light beings

The cosmic light supported the expansion of the core of the astral existence, the creation of the astral plane and sub-planes. The light was guided to create energy fields that will allow constant communication with the source. These energy fields were built prior to the creation of a plane and they continued to expand during the plane's creation and expansion.

The whole cosmic creation is supported by energy fields that allow the light, its powerful creative forces and the intention of the source to travel through planes and empower them with growth and transformation. All life is united and all energy fields are united carrying the light and the pure intention of the source. Life cannot be maintained and planes cannot grow without a system of unification that supports their ability to constantly exchange, receive and transmit light.

While the astral plane was expanding, the energy fields had to transform too. Everything that exists in the cosmos is a living being and its purpose is to support life, transform, grow and receive the light. All living beings follow cosmic laws and are tuned to the light that carries the intention of the source.

Light beings were created as an extension of the energy fields. There were energy points on astral fields that grew to have a unique purpose. They were able to support sub-planes and the connection with the astral plane and the light by creating micro fields that can be moved and adjusted according to growth processes.

It was necessary for light beings to carry unique gifts in order to support the vast and multi-layered organism, the astral plane, to create more sub-planes with unique purposes and abilities to create life.

Introduction

The cosmic unity and powerful connection between astral beings are supported by their ability to receive and transmit light. This helps them to constantly grow and supports the creation of energy fields that unite them, allowing the light to create within the cosmos. Astral beings do not have a body and mind purpose so they are fully disconnected from thoughts, beliefs, fear, drama, disappointment or failure. Their purpose is only to receive and transmit light, and grow with others for the light of the cosmos to create.

We all exist in unity and growth. This is our driving force to help us connect to the Source. When you understand that all beings are created to experience unity by receiving and transmitting light then you will experience the cosmos being part of yourself. We are all connected to each other and energy, which is information, passes from one body to another. If you have the skill to translate cosmic information and bring it to your own plane then you are a creator.

Wisdom of Thoth: Astral families

The cosmic unity and powerful connection between astral beings are supported by their ability to receive and transmit light. This helps them to constantly grow and supports the creation of energy fields that unite them, allowing the light to create within the cosmos. Astral beings do not have a body and mind purpose so they are fully disconnected from thoughts, beliefs, fear, drama, disappointment or failure. Their purpose is only to receive and transmit light, and grow with others for the light of the cosmos to create.

Astral beings have a strong connection to their astral family and share a common purpose. These connections carry purity, truth and the great power of creation that is shared by the cosmic light. When astral beings are called to reincarnate, they are supported by their astral family and all light beings are often part of the preparation needed for this to happen. When a light being reincarnates, the astral body still exists on the astral plane.

However, a reincarnation can bring some unique transformation to this light being as well as to its astral family. Often astral beings reincarnate together and form family connections, friendships and partnerships. Beings from the same astral family can have many reincarnations together and can reinforce ancestral patterns and connections to be experienced by humans. Light beings can reincarnate together and share a physical experience on Earth or have an energetic connection.

Members of the same astral family can connect in a brief way to bring light and guidance to each other. The light family supports the birth and the transition at the end of a life cycle for light beings that reincarnate. Due to the distortion on Earth, human beings find it challenging to connect to their path and the true guidance that is available to them and feel lost.

When humans disconnect from their true path, distortion affects all aspects of their life. It is possible that these special connections become polluted and create blockages in a being. Purification can support light beings to recognize astral family members who are reincarnating with them or want to guide them on their path.

Introduction

The following teaching will share wisdom about the creation of lower planes. The astral plane is a complex electromagnetic field and its energy occupies the greatest part of cosmic creation. It is an enormous, multidimensional energy space of transformation that is divided into many sub-planes of various energetic structures. It is the home of our astral body which is our permanent and eternal existence. There was a time that all beings, including Earth, experienced life only in the astral plane. The creation of physicality was a transformation of the astral body that was allowed to be experienced by a small number of astral beings. It was seen as a unique creation, leading to an extension of the astral plane.

Wisdom of Thoth: Creation in the lower planes

The light beings that exist in the astral plane have no beginning or end; they have unlimited opportunities for growth. They can receive and transmit constantly. This constant movement of light that brings life to all beings is the essence of the source.

The source is in constant movement, regeneration, and growth and this is why the qualities of its life and creation are constantly being renewed and its existence and ability to create have no beginning or end.

160

All beings that exist in the cosmos have a creation code and this is the seed of our Source that created their being. The creation code exists as part of the Source and is able to generate different forms of life that can expand and transform. These forms of life are created in the astral plane with the light of our Source and the creative powers of the divine light, working together as one to create life.

Before the creation of the physical body, Earth was a light being and supported the expansion of the astral plane, this means that she was a receiver and transmitter of light and supported life, growth, and higher light spreading to the astral plane for expansion and the creation of new life.

At this point, there was not a divine plan that Earth will have a physical body. She was supporting the power of cosmic light to create layers of cosmic existence so the astral plane can become a powerful laboratory of life.

The sub-planes that surrounded the astral plane supported its growth and its ability to create various energy fields and eventually become a complex organism. Some of the subplanes became planes that had different vibrations and started to exist as separate beings with their own laws and creation. The new planes were seen as a wonderful experiment, allowing new life to be created and new energy fields to be built.

Some of these planes became the home of a unique form of growth and transformation, the physical body. It was the Source's intention that the cosmic light travelled to all planes, bringing life to all energy fields and light beings. The cosmic light is always teaching you that there is unity in the cosmos and through unity there is growth.

Introduction

The astral plane went through a number of transformations when the lower planes were created. They were part of the astral but very soon developed their own ways to grow and transform, absorb the light, and create. All planes are living beings; they are part of the cosmic field and one of the main centers of this field is the astral plane.

The astral plane is a powerful receiver of the light of the Source and when it reaches cosmic creation, the light becomes the powerful creative force that can unite every energy point in the whole creation. When this happens the light of the Source

becomes the light of the cosmos.

Wisdom of Thoth: Physical creation in the lower planes

The creation of the physical body was a growth opportunity offered to the new planes in order to avoid a total separation from the astral plane as they enter a low vibrational existence. The creation of a physical body was seen as a unique transformation: life will not be experienced only in the form of an astral being but can also carry another form.

The physicality was a unique creation and the cosmic light was eager to create many different variations of this. What was created first by cosmic light is a physical plane. This was a space of creation where the divine and the cosmic light would unite to create a unique form of life and energy fields that can support its growth. This was seen as high growth and a great opportunity for the astral plane to grow.

The creative forces of the cosmos created new forms of life in the low planes. They were seen as a new laboratory where they could create life through unique processes that cannot be experienced in the astral plane. The light supported the formation of different types of physical life, starting with the creation of star systems and planets.

This was the time that the astral being Earth was called to agree to receive a physical body and experience life in the lower planes. At this phase of growth, the lower planes were seen as the most exciting, diverse, and powerful creation. This made many light beings want to receive a physical body.

Introduction

Earth and other light beings that existed in the astral plane were given an important role: to receive and transmit light to the sub-planes and support the growth, expansion and connection with the astral plane. These light beings were chosen to create a physical body. They went through a process of intense preparation to enter the new planes and countless powerful transformations that will initiate the creation of their physical body.

Wisdom of Thoth: A body in process of evolution

Earth was not the only living being that experienced a physical transformation; there were many other light beings that created their own physical body and formed these new planes that were an extension of the astral plane.

When a body is in a process of evolution, it is going to receive and generate more light. There is a great movement of energies, connecting to the cosmic light and also connecting to other beings and energetic forms. The movement supports growth and creation.

There was a constant movement that supported communication between the physical beings, connection with the astral plane, the high light of the Source, and the ability to accelerate growth in the new planes. The new planes needed balance and this was part of their growth.

The growth that was experienced in the new planes slowly took a different path from the processes of growth and creation in the astral plane. In the astral plane, everything exists in unity and individual growth is always supporting collective growth.

The creation of the new planes followed similar patterns but the diversity and uniqueness of the physical body led to a new form of individuality and uniqueness. This new form of growth was supported by new laws that allowed astral beings to create physical life in their own unique way. New groupings and divisions started to appear and multiple physical forms with their own unique characteristics were created on different planets and astral systems.

Introduction

In the golden era, all beings were fully connected to Earth and were able to participate in all processes of growth and transformation because they saw themselves as an extension of Earth's physical and astral body. Earth's creative force will allow them to be in constant regeneration and rebirth, receiving the highlight of the cosmos into their being and supporting the vast energy field that unites all life.

This type of creation was experienced in many planets and allowed them to slowly build their own natural laws, focus on unique processes of growth in order to support the creation, and experience some independence from the growth in the astral plane, following new planetary laws. Each planet had its own laws and they supported creation processes, the growth of individual life forms, ways to balance individual life forms, collective purpose and divine plan.

Wisdom of Thoth: An explosion of life on Earth

Earth's creation followed the astral laws initially and later there was an explosion of life that created many life forms. The whole physical body of Earth was created to nourish all these life forms. A point of high growth was experienced by Earth when she was able to create beings that were able to receive and transmit light. These beings carried the light of Earth's astral body and the physical body went through many transformations over the different cycles of growth. At this time there was not a clear distinction between animals, plants, water/land formations, or elements.

These high-energy beings will have certain privileges as well as duties: becoming creators themselves and sharing their light to support Earth's creation and growth. Earth will give responsibilities and engage all life in processes of growth and transformation in order to empower and link physical creation with the astral plane.

Earth's physical body was created by the light of the Source. The physical body went through many energy exchanges to receive the high light of creation that caused the birth of many different life forms.

The creation of life forms on Earth's physical body altered her creative intention and affected the balanced coexistence between all the beings that existed on the planet. Earth experienced an explosion of life in her whole physical body: a mixture of microorganisms, plants, animals, elements, waters, mountain formations, and entrances that will give access to all different layers of the whole Earth's body.

Introduction

Earth experienced the birth of her physical body as an extension of her astral being and she saw it growing, transforming, receiving the light of the cosmos, and eventually having a life of its own. The astral being Earth was observing the creation of the physical body and she directed the highlight of the cosmos into her physicality to support its growth and expansion. All light beings in the new planes that went through a transformation to experience a new form of existence, a physical body, was able to exist in both states, the physical and the astral.

Wisdom of Thoth: The Birth of Earth's core

The astral being Earth gave birth to the core of the planet that became her physical body. At that time all light beings that went through a transformation to experience a new form of existence, a physical body, were able to exist in both states, the physical and the astral.

Earth experienced the birth of her physical body as an extension of her astral being and she saw it growing, receiving the light of the cosmos, and eventually having a life of its own. Earth's core was a high vibrational planet ready to grow and experience life that was unique.

One of the important creations that were experienced by Earth was the grid which can also be seen as an extended energy field, covering all parts of her physical body as well as the energies that surround this physical body. This grid was created to support and protect the new physical being and to maintain a connection between the astral body and the physical body of Earth.

CHAPTER X

**If your energy is distorted, you create distortion
if you have illusionary beliefs, you are fearful, sad, angry,
disappointed, you blame others, you do not experience your
true state and path, you have an illusionary understanding and
experience of life and creation. This is a low vibrational state
that will not guide you to the golden era.**

Introduction

The astral plane exists in constant expansion and this supports the creation of many subplanes that became separate planes having their own vibration.

The lower vibrational planes allowed physicality and astral existence to co-exist. The high vibrational planes had a different purpose. Being highly vibrational, they can carry high light and offer an energy space for preparation leading to an initial phase of the creation that is going to happen in the astral plane. These high planes are the most powerful receivers and transmitters of light. They have great awareness of the light, its creative qualities and the plans of creation and often support and enhance the creative process.

Wisdom of Thoth: Fertile lands for high creation

The astral plane grew and created planes with high vibration to support further expansion needed for the astral plane to support the creation of life. These higher planes are pure spaces of powerful growth and transformation able to experience the creative abilities of light more than any other plane.

They are divided into sub-planes and the one that carries the highest vibration is the Pleroma. These higher planes can experience the intention of the source and how it is passed to the light that is going to create life in the astral plane. Because of these powerful connections, the high planes are able to be fertile lands for high creation.

The cosmic and divine light exists in this cosmic space and often high creation takes place there and then is transmitted to the astral plane to support its growth processes. The astral plane exists in unity with the high planes. We can explain this by using the analogy of the astral being and the higher self.

The high planes can offer a space for the light to go into a preparation process that may include multiple transformations. or allow the light to create an initial phase of the creation that is going to happen in the astral plane. The high planes are the most powerful receivers and transmitters of light. They have great awareness of the light, its creative qualities and the plans of creation and often support and enhance the creative process.

Introduction

The light in all beings is expanding in order to move to higher planes and finally connect to the Source. This is how creation grows and regenerates itself. All beings have a natural ability to grow to higher planes and the energy fields and grids support this growth. There is constant communication within your being, between you and your astral body, higher self, and creation code.

This communication can be seen as an energy exchange and creates countless opportunities for growth, guiding you on your path. All beings want to connect to the source because they want to renew the starting point of their creation. This can only happen when you connect to your creator and reestablish energetic communication.

Wisdom of Thoth: The purpose of high planes

Some of you may want to know more about the purpose of high planes, how they connect to each other and the astral plane. The seed of creation exists in the intention of the source and is placed in the core of the astral plane. The astral core carries all divine resources that can support the creation and expansion of the plane.

The astral plane is a living being whose constant expansion, growth and transformation support its eternal existence. It is constantly expanding to maintain life and light in its being. The high vibrational sub-planes were created during a series of powerful transformations and supported the effortless flow of light moving through the fields and light beings who supported new creation and expansion.

The new sub-planes offered the light a greater space to gather and go through preparation for creation. As the astral plane is expanding, the light will not always reach the core and spread to the rest of the astral creation. Instead, it will move through fields and light beings as well as reach the core all at the same time with greater power and clear purpose. The high vibrational planes offer light space for different phases of preparation to take place and support the light and the creative forces of the cosmos to continue creating a new life as well as maintaining eternal life.

Introduction

In this teaching, we learn about the creation of high energy fields. High energy fields are communicating with each other and the astral plane in order to support the light creating and maintaining life. The light will create high vibrational energy fields to support the flow of creation. The connection and communication between the high planes make the preparation effortless. The sub-planes of the astral plane experience high transformation constantly and the same is experienced by the living beings and the energy fields that support them.

Wisdom of Thoth: The creation of the high planes

Before the creation of the high planes, the divine and cosmic light created fields around the astral plane for possible expansion. These fields can be understood as the aura of the astral body. When the cosmic and the divine light received the intention of the source and guidance for the creation, they travelled to the energy field and remained there.

They went through a preparation that consisted of many transformations and then the light entered the astral plane with a divine plan. This divine plan will guide and support them to maintain or create life in the astral plane and the sub-planes. It was the intention of the source that high planes were created to support the preparation and new forms of communication between the source's intention and the astral plane.

Many higher vibrational planes were created and had a similar purpose. They were able to carry the light in its pure and powerful form and they had the ability to go through many transformations in order to fulfil their purpose. The living beings and the energy fields that supported their growth, had to go through many metamorphoses in order to maintain their ability to receive and transmit light.

High energy fields are communicating with each other. They are the steps of a unique and powerful preparation that supports the light to receive the guidance of the intention of the source and go into a transformation process that will create the next divine plan. The connection and communication between the high planes make the preparation effortless. These sub-planes experience high regeneration constantly and the same is experienced by the living beings and the energy fields that support them.

Introduction

The astral plane is a powerful receiver of the light of the Source and when the astral plane transmits it, the light becomes the powerful creative force that reaches every energy point in the whole creation. When this happens the light of the Source becomes the light of the cosmos. All planes are alive because of the light beings that support their growth. The creation of multiple sub-planes affected their ability to grow, receive and transmit light.

The light is a unifier and will never create separation because this restricts the life flow and creation. There are no restrictions, imbalances or blockages in the astral plane and the high vibrational planes. The abundance that exists in the being of the source is shared constantly with all beings through its intention, the cosmic and divine light that ignites and maintains growth for all cosmic unity.

Wisdom of Thoth: The light will never create separation

Everything in the cosmos exists in unity and this is how the light supports the growth of all creation. This cosmic law is experienced by all life in the cosmos, including light beings, planes, sub-planes and the creative forces of the cosmic and divine light.

Without cosmic unity, creation will not be possible; creation and creator are one in the cosmos. The source, its intention, the creative forces and all creation is one and coexist. There is communication between sub-planes and this is supported by energy fields and light beings who are placed in certain energy points to support unity.

If you try to understand this with your mind, you may come to the conclusion that there is a distinct separation between sub-planes related to vibration and purpose and you may be even tempted to number them or give them unique characteristics. All sub-planes are connected and this supports their communication and unity.

The light will never create separation because this restricts the life flow and creation. There are no restrictions, imbalances or blockages in the astral plane and the high vibrational planes. The abundance that exists in the being of the source is shared constantly with all beings through its intention, the cosmic and divine light that ignites and maintains growth for all cosmic unity. All living beings can receive and exist in the abundance of the Source. The cosmic law of unity supports the existence and growth of this special gift.

Introduction

When a body is in a process of evolution, it is going to receive and generate more light. There is a great movement of energies, connecting to the cosmic light and also connecting to other beings and energetic forms. The movement supports growth and creation. There was a constant movement that supported communication between the physical beings, connection with the astral plane and the high light of the Source, and the ability to accelerate growth in the new planes. The new planes needed balance and this was part of their growth.

Wisdom of Thoth: Constant Growth and Transformation

Light beings that were created in the astral plane by cosmic and divine light, can exist in sub-planes of higher vibration. They are supporting energy fields, the flow of light moving from one sub-plane to the other. The light beings that exist in these planes went through many transformations and have grown to carry and transmit light.

They become powerful portals for the light to connect to the source's intention and start creating following high guidance. All light beings become one with the energies, the light, the growth and creation experienced in their sub-plane and the purpose of their existence is shaped according to the purpose and growth of the sub-plane.

Some of you may ask: Will the astral plane expand eternally, creating more sub-planes and how can this affect creation? Growth phases, transformation and creation are cosmic processes that are going to happen constantly. The astral plane becomes stronger, carrying more light when it expands.

Transformation and growth are experienced by all beings in the cosmos. When high planes transform and expand, they support a more powerful connection with the source and a more clear direction regarding creation. The divine light and the cosmic light are able to support the countless growth processes that are happening in the cosmos and create a divine plan.

Introduction

In this teaching, you will learn about the purpose and creation of the divine plan.

The divine plan is a form of communication, a map of greatness, that supports all beings to tune into the source. Light beings when they reincarnate, they become aware of their divine plan which offers information and guidance about the purpose of their lifetime. Light beings receive the divine plan through the higher self which is an extension of their being and offers them the guidance that they need in order to fulfil their purpose. The divine plan travels to their whole being and enables them to connect to the collective purpose and growth.

Wisdom of Thoth: The divine plan

The divine plan of cosmic creation is the guidance that the light receives from the intention of the source and all beings in all planes when they receive the light, they also receive the divine plan. The divine plan is a map and a form of empowerment that affects the growth of all beings in the astral plane and the sub-planes. The divine plan is aware of the opportunities that living beings have to grow and is supporting these processes by communicating and guiding the cosmic light to enter their being and support transformations.

Light beings and planes experience collective growth; there are no divisions, separations or schisms. The cosmic law of unity supports constant growth to be experienced by all beings and this ability creates a common purpose and divine plan.

Light beings receive the divine plan through the higher self which is an extension of their being and offers them the guidance that they need in order to fulfil their purpose. The divine plan travels to their whole being and enables them to connect to the collective purpose and growth.

The divine plan is a form of communication, a map of greatness, that supports all beings to tune into the source. Light beings when they reincarnate, they become aware of their divine plan which offers information and guidance about the purpose of their lifetime. During the preparation and transition phase, light beings will receive the divine plan that will guide them through all transformations, opportunities of growth and experiencing their true gifts and path. The divine plan exists in your being and spreads to every part of you. It offers you the opportunity to experience unity within your being and enter the collective growth that supports Earth's creation.

Introduction

Do not be afraid of letting go of your current affairs, personal ambitions, competition, anger and desires; all these can only lower your ability to transform and become one with the gods and the divine plan. We are part of a renewal process that has started already in some spheres and will finally affect all. The main work will take place in the lower planes and will help people to adjust to the overall transformation where everything is linked and moving together at a faster pace. When humans are able to fight illusion and heal distortion, they will support the planet's growth and transformation. There are many people on Earth who are walking the path of awakening. Their numbers are going to grow; this is the divine plan.

Wisdom of Thoth: Abundance on Earth

Some of you may ask: is it important for human beings on Earth to be aware of their divine plan and how they can achieve this? Many people are not aware of their divine plan but they are also not aware of their being and all the natural processes that bring growth and transformation to your life on Earth.

Human beings are not able to disconnect from the mind and find their way into the truth that supports the path and their purpose in this lifetime. They cannot disconnect from illusionary beliefs, social expectations, addictions and survival fears. All these limitations create their reality and limit their understanding of their path and purpose.

Your divine plan is carried by your light that exists in the core of your being.

Your light is an extension of your astral existence and carries your divine plan, all truth about your unique gifts, path and purpose. Your light will guide you to connect with all the support available to you on Earth and open all doors in your being that bring in the support and light of Earth and creation in you so you can be a powerful receiver and transmitter of light.

When you achieve this and you make it your life focus, you become aware of your unique gifts and use them in your everyday life. This helps you to experience effortless greatness; you have immense clarity that is constantly leading you to the effortless flow of your path toward fulfilling your purpose; you discover new and powerful ways to heal yourself and others; you create with your light because you have purified yourself from impurities and imbalances. You are now able to expand beyond artificial and illusionary boundaries and obstacles. When you experience abundance and all-natural and cosmic resources available to you to continue with your everlasting growth then you are experiencing your divine plan.

Introduction

I want you to see the divine plan and understand that unity and constant evolution bring grace and peace. We understand grace as the power of the infinite; the power of the high creator gods. I want you to understand that even though you can take many forms, you are an infinite source of evolution that has no body and no thought.

All that you are is an energy field and countless other energy fields are connected to you all transforming at the same time, giving each other support, transmitting and receiving information, reaching out and creating life. I want you to understand the vastness of who you are and perhaps then you can understand that the five senses are a limitation to your understanding of your true purpose. Your true purpose is already known to you because its reflection is part of your energy field.

With our teachings, we want to wake you up, help you see beyond your everyday illusion. My duty is to continue teaching you. Your duty is to clear your path and find your purpose. I hope that you will continue learning from me. When you truly learn you will progress and clarity will be with you.

175

Wisdom of Thoth: Experiencing cosmic growth

Experiencing your divine plan you are opening yourself to a powerful experience and this is to live your life as a cosmic being. It will help you connect to the light within that is a powerful guide and creator that follows cosmic laws.

You will connect to the light of the cosmos that is fully aware of greater divine plans as they are created by the intention of the source and spread to all cosmic creation. These experiences are natural and cosmic processes that are available to all beings who experience reincarnation on Earth.

Human beings are never disconnected from astral growth and it is part of their purpose and path to bring astral growth to Earth. Their true purpose is not to experience a life of struggle, trauma, imbalances, fears and limitations. These can be experienced only when they move through diversions and distance themselves from their true path and power.

The divine plan does not point out these limitations because they do not truly exist. This truth can guide you out of such distortion and artificiality. If you give it your power it grows and if you purify and let it go, it shrinks and has no power over you. You are then free to experience your divine plan.

Introduction

Earth is a powerful creator and she is connected to the high light. She is eternal and in constant transformation. The divine plan for Earth's growth is going to affect the whole planet in a profound way.

All beings from the rock to the tiny plant, from the tallest tree to the biggest mammal and from the insect to the fish are micro vibrational fields. They produce their own energy and they are able to feed from the energy of the Earth and the cosmos. Their connection to high energetic fields keeps them alive and helps them to grow. All beings that vibrate on Earth are connected to the planet's energies. The divine plan for Earth's purification and growth is going to affect the whole planet in a profound way.

Wisdom of Thoth: Earth's divine plan

When human beings become aware of their divine plan, created to guide them through their reincarnation on Earth, they will also become aware of Earth's divine plan. Earth as a living being carries a plan that is supported by her light, her astral existence and her ability to fulfil her purpose as a powerful creator.

All living beings who reincarnate on the planet are going to grow and be aware of her divine plan. This is part of their purpose and is going to ignite their cosmic gift to experience life as a powerful receiver and transmitter of light. The energy of all living beings is supporting the energy grids of Earth.

This is how Earth maintains her cosmic gifts being a receiver and transmitter of cosmic light as well as constantly experiencing herself being a powerful creator. When human beings become aware of their plan, they start to expand enormously. They are aware of all the connections in their being related to growth and transformation.

They are able to connect to their being, their true path and their gifts with more clarity and purification. Healing becomes a natural process available to them at all times. They are growing in a space of abundance as they receive the light of the Earth. Cosmic guidance and support are spread by the light in them that carries the divine plan and all the pure intention for growth that is travelling through the energy grids of the cosmos and meeting the Earth grids.

Introduction

The creator exists in peace, which is a space of growth, when one does not experience competition, limitation, fear or survival. The creator knows that he does not own any of his qualities and gifts including the physical body. The creator is free from the need to own and possess. A creator is not affected by drama and artificial success. He is a person that connects to life and experiences life as a learning process and connection to the astral plane, the true home of all beings. Human beings that want to be creators, have to purify themselves from all imbalances and then connect to the high light.

When you connect to the high light, creation will happen naturally and you will see yourself and others being transformed because of it. When one creates, this affects its own light and understanding of the cosmos. It also affects all people who are connected to him. One of the qualities of light is to be able to spread, purify and transform all beings. All creation should be in a process of constant purification and transformation.

Wisdom of Thoth: Release the impure state

Experiencing your light, your divine plan and constantly expanding towards the cosmos and Earth, will definitely help you disconnect from limitations that support an illusionary and impure state and enter an ever-powerful state of abundance that spreads through all living beings and connects the Earth and the cosmos. Your divine plan is cosmic guidance to help you experience this.

There is abundance in you that spreads through the Earth and the cosmos because everything exists in unity and everything grows together at this moment, a moment that is created by the cosmic and divine light. You are called to experience your divine plan and the abundance that grows in you and then you will be called to experience the abundance that exists on Earth.

All the living beings that have reincarnated on Earth and are growing and sharing their light, at this present moment, are becoming aware of Earth's divine plan. It is their pure intention to grow with her, and support the abundance that is offered to her creation by sharing their own light. Living beings are ready to tune into Earth's natural processes of growth and experience them in their being.

Tuning to Earth's growth offers them the opportunity to experience her body, light, true purpose and her powerful gifts. Living beings are having deep connections and powerful exchanges with Earth and this supports collective growth. They are finally free from the limitations in the mind and are now transforming into powerful creators.

Introduction

You are not on your own; you belong to a high family that is constantly calling you to connect. We are here to guide you; your purpose is our gift and fits perfectly in the divine plan. When you connect to us you will experience transformation. We are sharing this knowledge with you because we want to break your chains from your distorted understanding of yourself.

You are a powerful being. Do not let fear block your way to receiving, transmitting and co-create. Show how passionate and ecstatic you are to be healed from your imbalances and offer this healing to others; to create a life close to Earth and allow nourishment and light to reach your physical body; to experience people growing with you and love you for your contribution to their process of growth. When unity is experienced by human beings, they will connect to their purpose and have an effortless life.

Wisdom of Thoth: Becoming a powerful creator on Earth

To become a powerful creator on Earth, you have to experience your divine plan because it carries all the truths about the purpose of your reincarnation. The truth will empower you and help you release all the blocks in your being. Your divine plan is guiding you to overcome limitations, to experience healing and love for everything that has allowed you to grow and have a fulfilling life.

Your divine plan is showing you a much bigger picture of the true understanding of everything around you. Your path, purpose, light, energy, opportunities for growth, your connection with Earth and the cosmos are all going to be marked on your divine plan. In this plan, you will not discover the impurities, imbalances and all forms of distortion that can be found on Earth.

The plan will not include the problems, obstacles and challenges in your life and will not show you the events that brought destruction into your life. The divine plan will show you the perfection in you. You were created to be perfect, powerful and constantly connected to the cosmic light. You were created to share your perfection and create greatness with it. You were created to grow in perfection and see it as your only state of existence. You follow your divine plan and you connect with the intention of the source.

Introduction

The cosmic laws bring harmony, balance and connection. They control and balance all the energies and forces in the cosmos. We are taught by the source that there is a divine pattern in all beings. There is a structure that helps the light of the creator come to you, balance your energy and give life. We are all part of an eternal divine plan.

All creation is unified. We all receive and transmit light. We are all creators and we have the tools to maintain balance not only in us but also in all beings that are connected to us. When the inhabitants of a planet suffering from a disease that affects the balance and their light, this means that the planet is also suffering from the same disease. The illusion and fragmentation are the symptoms.

I am calling all people on Earth who want to banish the impurity of illusion, and restore wholeness and perfection, to connect to the light of the gods. You are never too far away from your purpose.

As we are all connected to the divine plan, we are all growing together and the people of Earth will be able to expand according to the form of their higher self. I am here to show you the way and with you, to build bridges between the Earth and the Pleroma. This is an opportunity for you to start growing again.

Wisdom of Thoth: The perfection of the cosmic creation

A divine plan shows all the perfection of a cosmic creation and this is why it is a powerful guide to be experienced by all beings. It carries the pure intention of the source, the essence of powerful creative forces such as the cosmic and the divine light.

It carries the truth about all cosmic laws, the way living beings experience life, expansion and growth. The divine plan brings unity within the being to understand its potential and it also supports unity between the being and all life. This is a powerful part of creation; when all living beings unite and support collective growth, they can connect to the intention of the source.

Human beings on Earth are called to experience their divine plan at the core of their being. They are called to experience all connections, all guidance, all cosmic truths and all growth processes to help them create in their lives the perfection of their divine plan. This opportunity is always there for them and will remain until the end of their life cycle. Cosmic creative forces are designing the divine plan to be a high process of growth and transformation; another powerful guidance sent by the cosmos to all beings who are tuning in to the greatness and perfection of our source.

Introduction

It is important that you discover your true purpose and have a good understanding of how to use your tools and special gifts. When you have disconnected from the illusion and you are able to see yourself naked and pure, then you will instantly see your purpose; you will have instant access to all cosmic truths because it is your right. Cosmic creation does not wish to hide cosmic wisdom from humans or deny them the empowerment of the high vibrational state.

Cosmic truths are reaching all humans as they connect to the divine and cosmic light. We want humanity to wake up in order to assist the planet in waking up too. Earth and her creation suffer from the same disease and this is a schism of the true self and the growth of illusion. When you awake to the truth you will be restored to your true self.

Wisdom of Thoth: Human beings connecting to the intention of the Source

Some of you may ask: Is it possible for human beings on Earth to experience the source's intention and create their life being tuned to its intention? When all life is supported by the cosmic and divine light and is nourished by the everlasting greatness of the source; when all life exists in unity in order to remain nourished by the supreme greatness that cannot be detected or explained by the mind of living beings on Earth; the focus of growth in all planes lies with all living beings connecting to the source. It is true that all living beings are growing, focussing on their connection and expansion toward the source.

We are now supporting humanity to focus on the light within, experience the divine plan and grow towards the absolute connection with the source.

Let the light clear imbalances and limitations. Create a space for the light to expand in your being.

Focus on the core of your existence and meet your own light and divine plan, your own perfection. Remain in this space in unity with the light. It will guide you to become a creator. When you create with the light and your life is the divine plan, then you are expanding toward the greatness and perfection of the source.

Introduction

The unity that exists in the cosmos is contained in the light of our creator and is spread to the creation through our creation code. Our unity with our creator is a high truth and when we are able to understand the wisdom, we will open ourselves to the possibility of being a creator.

The astral plane is your home and there you spend the longest period of your existence. In that state, you receive guidance from your higher self and divine intervention from your creation code. Your astral body is aware of your purpose and growth cycles; cosmic truth and wisdom go through the astral body in the form of energy and this is why the astral body is in a process of constant purification and transformation. Unity and growth shape the astral existence of all beings.

Your astral body exists in you; you can always experience an expression of it in your physical plane and you are affected by its growth. You are one with your astral body and all the other parts of your being are connected to form one unit of light. You are light which we also call energy and because you exist in a multidimensional space, this unit of light takes many forms in different realms simultaneously.

Your being is a sea of light expanding from continent to continent but it is also a single drop. This is the greatness of our source, able to create many levels of growth and evolution.

Wisdom of Thoth: Connecting to the light

Some of you may ask what is the connection between the light of the gods, divine light, and the source? How does the source empower the divine light to create life and support cosmic growth? You will not be able to understand or experience the cosmos with an analytical mind who loves separation.

To understand the connection and exchange between the source and the divine light, you have to experience unity within your being. All parts of your being united carry the life flow. The same is happening in the cosmos: all living beings exist in unity as they carry the life force, the cosmic and divine light.

All living beings and all creative forces that support growth in the cosmos exist in unity and are part of the tremendous cosmic flow of creation. This flow of creation is never disconnected from the source; instead, it experiences cosmic abundance, growth and transformation within the light of the source.

Human beings may think that their physicality, mind, lifestyle and opportunities separate them from others but when they connect to the truth that they carry, they will be taught that they are also part of the cosmic flow that experiences cosmic abundance and unites them with the source.

When human beings experience this they will be liberated from the burden of distortion that wants them to believe that in order to understand the world around them, they have to be afraid of every representation of it and divide it into lots of different categories and classifications in order to win the survival battle. Now you have the opportunity to observe the immense power of the cosmic flow to unite all life and the ability of distortion to create schisms in your mind.

Introduction

The divine light can only exist connected to the source, absorbing its light and intention and moving towards the planes to create following the source's intention. The divine light has a resting light space and this is beyond the higher planes. The pleroma is a light space where divine light grows, transforms, receives cosmic light and nourishes its being in the abundance of the light of the source.

The Pleroma is a multidimensional, electromagnetic point in the universe, unseen by other beings. It is a secure temple where the creator gods can be in the right energies to enable them to connect to other gods and the creator. The Pleroma is in constant transformation following the transformation of the gods.

Building bridges between the Pleroma and Earth will help you experience transformation: you will be able to free yourselves from all negativity, pain, limitations and confusion. For this to happen you have to be open to the light of the Pleroma.

Wisdom of Thoth: The temple of the divine light

The divine light can only exist connected to the source, absorbing its light and intention and moving towards the planes to create, following the source's intention. The divine light has a resting light space and this is beyond the higher planes. It is a space where divine light grows, transforms, receives the cosmic force and nourishes its being in the abundance of the light of the source.

The divine light recognizes this space as the beingness of the source and this immense and immeasurable abundance of the divine light has built its home and its space of growth. Some human beings have named this light space the Pleroma trying to present and explain the totality, the fullness, the absolute perfection and the greatest abundance that is the being of the source and the divine light is not only experiencing this but they rest and grow in this space.

You may ask why all living beings cannot enter the Pleroma. This space is not created for all beings to enter because the growth and transformation that is experienced there, cannot be experienced in the astral plane or its sub-planes. Immense transformations are constantly changing the landscape of the pleroma and this supports the growth experienced by the divine light.

These powerful transformations that are unique to the pleroma, support the growth of unique gifts and abilities that can be experienced by the divine light so it can be the most effective creative force. The divine light is in communication with the intention of the source and can transform in order to receive the cosmic light and create it in all planes.

Introduction

In this teaching, you are going to learn more about the pleroma and its connection with the divine light and the source. The pleroma is a high vibrational state that is created by the energies of the divine light and the intention of the source. It is the state of absolute perfection that all beings want to reach on their quest to connect to the source. The pleroma maintains absolute purity and perfection by transforming constantly, following the growth of the divine light and supporting connections with the source.

Wisdom of Thoth: The pleroma is in constant transformation

Human beings would like to know more about the pleroma and perhaps compare it with their stories and mythologies related to the gods' abode.

For the divine light, the pleroma is a high vibrational state that is in direct connection with the source. It is created by the energies of the divine light and the intention of the source. The divine light goes through constant and powerful transformations in order to connect to the cosmic light and receive guidance from the source. The pleroma is supporting these transformations and it experiences them. Pleroma and divine light have the unique ability to transform and grow in unity.

This high vibrational state is part of the being of the divine light and other living beings cannot enter or experience it. The pleroma is the absolute perfection that all beings want to reach on their quest to connect to the source. It maintains absolute purity and perfection by changing form constantly, following the growth of the divine light and supporting connections with the source.

When the divine light is ready to communicate with the intention of the source and create, great regeneration and growth processes will be experienced by the pleroma: it will grow and expand towards the light of the source and create portals for communication to take place.

Introduction

All powerful connections, all transformation and growth processes, all expansion and opportunities are created by the divine light. The astral plane will continue to expand and grow and all sub-planes will connect to the astral plane through the powerful cosmic forces and will grow with it. All living beings are supporting the unity and the cosmic flow spreading to all living beings and all planes.

During her transformations, Earth was always surrounded and supported by the light of the Source, the intention of the gods, and other creative forces that are active in the astral plane and the sub-planes. The core was the first form of physicality that Earth has ever experienced and she always accepted it as her true physical body and all other parts as an expansion of the core. The gods created a new divine plan for

Earth and gave her new abilities to create so her physical form could expand. She understood her purpose as a creator and saw this as a great gift.

Wisdom of Thoth: Powerful opportunities for creation

The divine light exists in constant communication with the source and has the ability to support all major structures in the cosmos and the growth of all living beings. The divine light is an energy flow of great creation that is moving from the pleroma, to the core of the astral plane and all sub-planes in order to create life. The divine light is in constant transformation in order to travel to all planes and bring the guidance of the source to all living beings.

In the first phases of the growth of the astral plane, the cosmic flow that supported and guided the astral plane was the divine light connecting to the cosmic light. The divine light will create cosmic laws to balance creation. The divine light will create according to the cosmic laws and tune all creation to grow in a space of unity.

Creation happens when cosmic light unites with divine light. Their union carries the power of the source to create in all planes and support life to grow. The divine light directs the cosmic light to create following cosmic laws and the guidance from the intention of the source.

All planes with their energy fields and the living beings that support their expansion are in constant growth because of the unity of the divine and cosmic light reaching their being. This powerful creative flow can be experienced in the astral plane constantly and without interruptions or limitations.

All powerful connections, all transformation and growth processes, all expansion and opportunities are created by the divine light as it is communicated to them by the source. The astral plane will continue to expand and grow and all subplanes will connect to the astral plane through the powerful cosmic forces and will grow with it. All living beings are supporting the unity and the cosmic flow spreading to all living beings and all planes.

CHAPTER XI

The light of the Gods is everywhere in every being that is created by the high light of our source. The whole cosmos is our source, his expression of high light and naturally we are all longing for each other and our source. Our growth is our unity with our source. Strengthening our light and going through a transformation are the steps we take to achieve unity. See yourself at the crossroad, look at your path, look at your different paths and with truth and freedom move on and achieve unity.

Dialogue with Thoth

We received several questions from order members and students and below we present a dialogue between Thoth and humanity.

Question

There are many theories on Earth around the concept of words and how they manifest reality. Can Thoth please share some insight into how we might learn to communicate more truthfully? Are there different outcomes to reality based on the words we choose? For instance, many believe they must refrain from speaking in "foul" language as they believe this is somehow negative in some sense or creates negative outcomes in their life. I am curious about these things.

I will admit I sometimes find myself trying to share my own truth and feeling very misunderstood or poorly received. So in some ways, I do see how carefully chosen words can help with the inherent problems many have in communicating. But how important are words and the vibrations they carry?

Answer

Manipulators have created a science called public speaking, advertising, and teaching using repetitions of words and creating certain structures. The way you speak and the terms you use can create an illusionary space of fear, satisfaction, truth or freedom in people's minds and then they are ready to accept manipulation as a true aspect of their being. If human beings want to speak to others, express their true-self and pass the light of the cosmos and Earth then they have to use an authentic expression and allow their truth to become a bridge to help them exist in unity with others.

For this to happen you have to connect to your truth in your everyday experience, you have to communicate with pure intention and allow the cosmic light to be the main source of communication. You can also communicate what you are creating, with your learning. Or just being in peace connecting to your whole being. Do not rely on words for communication but when you have to speak then do it without restrictions, limitations or fragmentation. Communicate your truth in a way that is unique to you and expresses your ability to grow.

Question

Do low beings have a purpose on Earth? Why are they created and are they part of the source?

Answer

The collective of low energies that affect human beings and make them go against their own growth can be seen as unpurified energy that exists close to Earth's atmosphere. This unpurified energy once existed in a physical body. At the end of a life cycle, all beings have to go through a process of purification. For some, this process is so complex that it cannot be completed and this energy still exists in the Earth's atmosphere and is not able to return to the astral plane. This energy can manipulate, pollute, and feed on human beings on Earth. They manipulate people's minds by planting thoughts of fear, confusion and limitation or sometimes they appear as powerful light beings that have absolute control of life on Earth. If you have experienced this you have to understand and accept that these beings are part of Earth's distortion and as Earth is purifying from this you have to do the same. When you have healed yourself and purified your whole being, connecting to the light then this distorted energy will have no power to enter your being.

—————--------------------------------------

Question

Can you provide more information on different consciousnesses both on earth and beyond? Do other planets for instance have a similar problem with this parasitic type of consciousness that is here on Earth?

Answer

Consciousness is not the distortion that people on Earth experience in their everyday life. It is not the illusion that spreads through their mind and the fear patterns. Consciousness highlights your ability to grow and everything that you carry in you that supports this growth. The distortion that affects the human mind is not the greatest force on Earth. There is high growth therefore high consciousnesses on Earth that are helping this planet to create life and expand her energy field. It seems that the consciousnesses of humanity are not identical to the consciousnesses of Earth.

This is why humanity should stop focusing on Illusionary and harmful ways of living and go back to Earth and be taught by her. The people who accept the importance of truly connecting to Earth and allow her to teach them how to grow on the planet will understand Earth's consciousness and this will become their consciousness. It is interesting that the people who are demonstrating, complaining, and spending a lot of their time trying to save Earth, also exist in a maze of distortion and illusion. All these people have to stop arguing and create communities where they can truly connect to Earth and grow with her.

Question

I have been wondering about the effects of radiation on our planet and our health. What does this interference, 3g, 4g, 5g smart metres etc. that we are surrounded by do to our frequencies and does this create distortion in our energy field?

Answer

Human beings are not created to be affected by distortion of any kind. If they are able to connect to Earth's energies and the cosmic light, understand their purpose and create a life of truth then distortion cannot reach them. People who try to manipulate humanity and lock them into a space of limitation, have a powerful weapon and this is fear. Being afraid of possible disasters and how pollution and artificiality can affect your growth is much more harmful than the pollution itself. Focusing on your truth and light you can bring your divine plan into your life and raise your vibration by living behind distortion.

Energy flows through all beings throughout the cosmos. Energy is information and the purest way of communication. Everything in the universe is in constant transformation and movement. Nothing stays the same and there is no need to concentrate on the specific form but on the process of transformation. When there is transformation, the universe is alive and produces high energy able to sustain life.

Question

Can we reincarnate as an animal plant or mineral and what are the elementals?

Answer

All philosophies are ideas that have a purpose to offer some explanation or definition. Explanations are divisions and polarities; human beings worship their intellect and move away from experiencing the living truth in them. Even philosophies of non-duality carry a seed of separation. There are people on Earth who are wondering about reincarnation and if it is possible for a human being to have the opportunity to reincarnate as an animal or plant? Reincarnating as a human being does not define the opportunities for transformation that are coming your way. There is unity on Earth and great power for creation. This allows her to create a great number of species that are all growing and transforming together, supporting Earth's growth cycles.

For Earth, there are no divisions between the species of her creation and there is no hierarchy. These forms of separation exist in the mind of human beings and are reflected in their ideas and philosophies. Human beings understand the world around them as a complex pyramid structure and Earth wants to teach every single species, about unity and collective growth. The answer to your question about reincarnation will bring unity into your being. Light beings can reincarnate and experience the life of any species that exist on Earth.

Question

How can we protect ourselves from entities in the astral realm that wants to feed off of us energetically, if they exist? Especially at night while sleeping. Thank you

Answer

There are non-physical beings that carry low vibrational energies and feed from the energy of living beings on Earth. These beings exist in the Earth's energy field and experience a constant survival state trapped in a low vibrational existence. They had a lifetime on Earth but they were not able to complete the purification process that will enable them to return to the astral plane.

These beings support distortion, illusion, limitation, confusion, fear and disease in a being. These impurities create open doors for these beings to enter and feed from your energy. They can affect your mind when you are fearful and can lock you in a state of high anxiety; they affect people with addictions; they feed from people who are confused, following the same destructive patterns; they affect people who are not aware of their gifts and path and turn them against others, supporting the survival state. These beings can affect people in their sleeping state creating anxiety dreams and feeding from their energy. To protect yourself from these beings you have to exist in a state of peace and experience your true gifts and path. Bring peace into your being, nourish your body, follow your path and share your light unconditionally. All the above raise your vibration and you close your doors to the low beings.

—--

Question

The source's intentions are beyond our perception? Do we even get a glimpse? Are we just supposed to play our part? Do we connect to the source through the Gods?

Answer

Human beings or any other being in the cosmos are not designed to understand the intention of our source but they are designed to experience it. This can be achieved by connecting to your truth and becoming the creator of your life, following the path of growth. Human beings have to focus on their own path if they wish to connect to the cosmos that is the creation of our source.

Do not let the river of confusion and limitation take you away from connecting to your truth and become a perfect transmitter and receiver of cosmic light. People's minds are full of thoughts that are not supporting their purification, growth and creation. When you disconnect from illusionary thinking and acting then you will be able to find the path of your purpose and experience cosmic creation on Earth.

—--

Question

Many people use any variety of herbs and woods and grasses as a medium for burning and making smoke for the purpose of "cleansing".

I know these materials and other forms of incense have been used for a long time in many cultures throughout time. Many healers still use these natural materials in their rituals and ceremonies and claim they have abilities for purification. Some say burning sage can clear a house of bad spirits.

I would like to learn more about the truth regarding such practices.

Answer

Many people use smudging to purify a space but what they achieve is to stay connected with the low energies. It is not the space that needs purification but it is the being that has to disconnect from low energies. A being can pollute a space when it is connected to them and this way can affect other people. Smudging has no power to purify space.

In the past, this type of activity was used to attract low energies. When people breathe in the smoke they can be in a less conscious state. They believed that the physical body is a limitation and if they truly want to connect to the energies they have to be in a sleeping state or unconscious state. The use of hallucinogenic plants served the same idea. If you want to purify a space you should purify the people who live there.

Question

Who built the pyramids in Giza and who built the pyramids in Bosnia? The carbon-dated organic material from pyramids in Bosnia from underground chambers was dated to 39 600 years old. What races lived on Earth at those times, the races that we're able to build structures that we cannot reproduce?

Answer

In the golden era, Earth created natural pyramids of different materials that could carry and transmit energy such as crystals or stones and scattered them in many different locations on the surface of the planet as well as in the inner layers. These pyramids were receivers and transmitters of light and energy and supported the unity, growth and transformation of all layers of the Earth, tuning them to the powerful core. The pyramids were also used as a tool of communication between planets and energy exchange as well as to establish a connection between the physical, energetic and astral body of Earth.

When the first astral visitors arrived on the planet, they looted and partly destroyed these pyramids. Earth civilizations that were established after the golden era, understood the importance of these structures and they built their own pyramids or restructured the ones that were created during the golden era. Many civilizations built countless pyramids of all sizes around Earth decorated with precious stones and crystals. The pyramids of Egypt are a structure that was rebuilt multiple times by different civilizations from the period of the golden age to a few thousand years before the present time. The main pyramid is the oldest and the other ones were built at a later time. During the golden era, there was no technology, there was intention. Life is created because of the intention of the creator. Civilizations that existed after the golden era, used some technology to recreate the pyramids of the golden era. These technologies were far more advanced than the ones of the present time because they used energies and movement. There are many pyramids scattered around Earth and they are all related to the first pyramids built by Earth during the golden era.

———--

Question

How is life after death for us? Talking about my purpose in life, how do I know what I'm doing according to this purpose? Can I have access to my creation code while on this physical plane? How???

Answer

Life after death is not the same for every being but you have to see death as a new cycle of evolution connected to your life cycle. People reincarnate in order to achieve a high level of understanding and when they achieve that the physical body is resolved and all experiences and learning are stored in the astral body. The being then continues to evolve at a higher speed in the astral body. Beings that did not achieve progress and were not able to fulfill their purpose in this lifetime, will have a different path. Some of them are responsible for creating imbalances in their lives and energy as well as the life and energy of others. These people do not make progress; being in a confused state they are responsible for harming themselves and others. You need to understand that evolution takes place but it does not always produce the right result. So beings that had a non-effective evolution, after death have to purify themselves before they return to the astral plane. This purification balances the energy of the being and strengthens its light. After purification, beings return to the astral plane and often reincarnate again.

People on Earth are very confused. One of the main reasons for this is their fragmentation. They want to know their purpose but they live their lives according to people's expectations and demands. This is a schism that brings confusion and uncertainty. If you are able to block everything that is not your true self and distance yourself from the ideals of others, then you will instantly know what your purpose is and you will follow it because it is the only truth. Truth feeds you because it is the light that has created you. When you know your truth you will never go back to illusion; you will never have questions and you will live in harmony with everything that exists. You have reincarnated to prove that even in the deepest fog you can find your way. This is your challenge.

The creation code is part of the source and it exists in a safe place. Nobody, including yourself, can have access to your creation code.

———---

Question

There are so many innocent children and others that are ill and hungry and that die daily. Are those people that are living without basic needs all unenlightened and not worthy of enlightenment or life?

Answer

In the time of the Golden Era Earth's creation was able to feed from the light of the cosmos and the nutrients that were stored on the planet. Having long life cycles without disease, fragmentation, pain, negativity and experiencing constant growth was a natural process. This was supported by Earth, the planet creator, her guides the Gods of the Pleroma and the beings that lived on her. All these different aspects of life on Earth supported evolution and they were the receivers and transmitters of light. Looking at the present time we see on Earth fragmentation, distortion and schism; they affect Earth's growth and the growth of her creation. Earth is not always able to safeguard her resources. She is not always able to give shelter and nourishment to her creation because she is suffering from distortion. A reflection of the Earth's state can be seen in the life patterns of human beings.

You experience a hierarchy and a system of duality. High quality food and shelter is often related to high income or high status. Everybody needs nutrients that come directly from the Earth but this becomes an advantage for a small group of people on the top of the financial pyramid.

It seems that people with low income do not have the chance to nurture themselves but this is not true.

It is an illusion, it is a way to manipulate the masses and keep people in a low vibrational state. Bring yourself closer to Earth, be aware of her light and open yourself to receive her grace. Trust your connection with her and let her nourish you. Allow the creator-planet to share her light and create in you and then you produce light and create in your life and others. Cultivate your own plants, help others and share what you produce. If you open your eyes and be able to listen to your true self you will find many solutions and ways to connect to Earth. You can be free from illusion only if this is your intention.

Question

Is love one of the cosmic laws? Do astral beings experience love in the astral plane and how does it support their growth?

Answer

Human beings on Earth are called to experience unconditional love which supports co-creation, co-existence, exchange and unity. Unconditional love can create powerful bonds within a being; it can bring healing, clarity, inspiration, ability to connect to the light and transmit light. Unconditional love cannot coexist with the limitations of the mind; it supports the human being to exist in a pure state without attachments, needs, confusion, obstacles and struggles. Unconditional love guides human beings to their pure state and true path. You can experience this when you disconnect from all illusions that hold you back, when you love others with generosity and acceptance. Dive into your being, find your truth and greatness and share it with all beings on Earth.

Astral beings experience a powerful cosmic law and are called unity. They all grow in unity, sharing light and supporting growth in each other's being. Astral beings do not experience thoughts, emotions, mind or physicality. They exist in a pure state and the only focus is the path that unites them with all life.

———--

Question

I see myself trying to get in touch with myself and live an authentic, purposeful life, which I find very challenging. Your videos and articles are inspiring, although I caution myself from jumping too quickly into something. Where do you recommend going next?

Answer

Thank you for joining this space of truth. First, you need to ask yourself what you mean by the phrase "trying to get in touch with myself" How do you connect to yourself and what is the true purpose of this connection? How far away are you from illusion and what do you do to help and inspire others to find their own paths? Many people on Earth try to wake up but they find it a challenging task and sometimes misleading. You think you are awake but you still maintain old blockages. You think you are following your path but you are still suffering from insecurities and fear. I can show you the way to truth and it is a clear path, easy to find and easy to follow: connect to everything that is true in you and disconnect from all artificialities, insecurities and illusionary realities. Observe your life and find out what gives you true power to create and help others. It may be certain qualities, abilities, skills, or understanding that you have. These qualities can help you experience true life and when you are free and open to cosmic light you will be powerful and this power will be directed to others who are waiting to be free too. Follow the path of truth, this is the only way.

———--

Question

I do have a question and would like to receive clarity because of this what I have read in the "Higher Self" teaching. I require truth and wish to understand what the thoughts of Thoth are on energy work. I mean exactly Robert-jan, burning candles, herbs, adding oils, crystals and the like, or even creating the energy grids from crystals and doing it with a certain intention and/or asking for help or guidance and all of that. I would like to know if this is effective or if it is an illusion. I ask for more clarity as the teaching does say, "it was the search for his fine line which made humans practice magic and study occult teachings". Do these things fall within that category I suppose that is what I am asking? Thank you so very much for your answer.

Answer

In a low vibrational reality, human beings accept and believe that they are limited. They have many unanswered questions, they do not have clarity and also they identify themselves with the physical body and the decay that takes place during their life cycle. There are people who want to be leaders and want to control Earth and humanity. The ones who experience weakness and the ones who want power are going to find ways to empower themselves but they do not know that they both go on a diversion away from truth. There are people who think that if they are surrounded by certain crystals, burning oils and incense, praying, wearing certain clothes and holding certain objects are going to experience growth that will unite them with their astral body. There are many treasures on Earth to help you feed your being but purification, transformation and growth have to do with you knowing yourself, being able to observe yourself, being truthful, disconnecting from all negativity and letting go of your imbalances. Being surrounded by powerful crystals that can receive and transmit light can help you meditate but purification is your task and duty. There are people who focus on different materials thinking that they can achieve healing and growth. There are other people who give their powers away to forces whose intention is not known. Giving your power or being passive and waiting for a miracle are both illusionary and often destructive acts. If you wish to know yourself, fulfil your purpose and grow you have to disconnect from illusion and be brave to face your imbalances and limitations.

Question

Why do we not stay grounded all of the time without having to plan, or practice or think about it?

Answer

You are describing human nature when it is affected by distortion, people wearing a blindfold and believing they are truly blind. If people were able to connect to their truth, see their divine plan and purpose on Earth, accept their duty as a receiver and transmitter of light and connect to the cosmos and Earth, they will be able to see again.

Human beings do not only have one blindfold; they are as many layers of distortion in their being. Some people have to purify from fear by allowing the cosmic light to enter their being. You may have to observe the repeated patterns in you that have blocked you from connecting to the Earth and the cosmos. Do not see yourself as a limitation but as a seed that is growing to become a tree. Experience inner joy, truth and freedom and let them take you on a journey to growth.

————-------------------------------------

Question

Blessings to all! I have a question. What is the school of thought regarding starseeds and the concept of incarnations from other planets? I have had a few readings and they all have come up with Arcturian and Andromeda. I am a bit on the fence about it and I was just wondering if it is worth exploring.

Answer

There are many theories that try to bring light to the mechanics of reincarnation and some people try to link reincarnation with extraterrestrial life. All planets are part of the physical plane which is an extension of the astral plane. All living beings that reincarnate have the opportunity to have a life cycle on Earth or any other living planet. The physical body is created by the planet by energies, elements and creative forces that the planet has developed. At the end of reincarnation, the body remains on the planet and the being in a form of light returns to the astral plane and astral body. If the astral body is going to be involved in another reincarnation including a life experience on a certain planet then the light of the astral body will enter the new physical body. A new path, purpose, guides, support, healing and nourishment will be created for this experience. At the end of a life cycle, the body will remain on the planet and the light once again will join the astral body.

If human beings on Earth are drawn to life on other planets it may be happening because they had many reincarnations on these planets and they are connecting, communicating or being guided by these experiences. Past lives on Earth or other planets can support you in your current lifetime to help you connect to your path and purpose or develop your gifts. You can be open to all these experiences but also focus on remaining grounded and fully experiencing your life on Earth.

———--

Question

I have a question. Since Earth is in a state of misalignment; is it not due to us (humans) abusing Her? How can She come back into balance when humans continue to abuse the planet so viscously? Would it not be a continuous cycle of healing and destruction?

Answer

Earth's healing and transformation process requires that all life in all zones (from the core to the surface) receiving and transmitting light, are aware of their powerful abilities and path, exist in unity with Earth's body and are in constant growth and transformation with her. Earth's potential for growth is limitless when her whole being exists in the light.

When humans pollute the planet, they have accepted distortion as their path; they do not recognize their ability to receive and transmit light and experience a low vibrational state. When people are in a self-destruction mode, they recognize life as a constant fight for survival and not as a cycle of growth. This interrupts or slows down Earth's growth cycle. All beings on the planet are given opportunities to grow with Earth and support her to heal and transform. Many living beings are tuned to her light and have become co-creators with her. Human beings on the surface are one of the many species that Earth has created. When human beings will start to experience unity with Earth's creation and observe the powerful receivers and transmitters, they will move a few steps away from distortion and into Earth's light.

Question

Are we (humanity) supported by Galactic federation (alliance) and Ashtar command to facilitate ET disclosure and transition into Golden age/ Ascension to the higher realities of unity and love?

Answer

Alien intervention and ET disclosure in all their forms are only distractions affecting the mind and the emotions of human beings and dragging them into a state of confusion. Theories and beliefs related to the coming of alien super races, creators of advanced technology and high consciousness, who are ready to solve all problems, can distract people from experiencing their true path and the true purpose of their current lifetime.

When people speak about alien intervention, they are presenting unresolved mysteries of the past or the future that are open to different interpretations, theories, fantasies, stories, beliefs and agendas. Theories about alien intervention make people experience strong emotions such as fear, hope or they can go on a roller coaster of emotions. The alien agenda can support polarities, separation and divisions between the good and the bad, superior and inferior. All these elements can create fascinating stories that distract and block people from one truth. When human beings connect to truth, they experience peace and peace can be found in the present moment. Human beings should focus on what is truly important to help them grow in the present moment. Human beings will experience their power and greatness when they know the purpose of this lifetime.

Question

Is love one of the cosmic laws? Do astral beings experience love in the astral plane and how does it support their growth?

Answer

Human beings on Earth are called to experience unconditional love which supports co-creation, co-existence, exchange and unity. Unconditional love can create powerful bonds within a being; it can bring healing, clarity, inspiration, ability to connect to the light and transmit light. Unconditional love cannot coexist with the limitations of the mind; it supports the human being to exist in a pure state without attachments, needs, confusion, obstacles and struggles. Unconditional love guides human beings to their pure state and true path. You can experience this when you disconnect from all illusions that hold you back, and when you love others with generosity and acceptance. Dive into your being, find your truth and greatness and share it with all beings on Earth.

Astral beings experience a powerful cosmic law and which is called unity. They all grow in unity, sharing light and supporting growth in each other's being. Astral beings do not experience thoughts, emotions, mind or physicality. They exist in a pure state and the only focus is the path that unites them with all life.

Question

Is the astral plane connected to our reality (3rd dimension, 3rd density) to serve for recycling the souls that reincarnate on Earth? Or is the Astral plane a "meeting" non-physical place where the souls can choose their next steps?

Answer

The astral plane is a space of creation; it is the home of all life. All living beings are created in the astral plane and they all exist in the form of an astral body. This is a constant, everlasting and high growth existence of all beings. Reincarnation is not a necessary or frequent experience for astral beings and when it happens it is only a short cycle of growth in their everlasting and limitless existence in the astral plane. When beings reincarnate, the astral body continues to exist. The process of reincarnation allows light from the astral body to enter the physical body that is created in the womb and the light becomes the cosmic seed in the core of the new being. The soul is also light coming from the astral body and supports the connection between the physical and the astral body as well the movement and transition of the light moving in or leaving the physicality at the end of the Earth's life cycle. The light and the soul return to the astral plane and reunite with the astral body.

Astral bodies are in constant transformation and growth, constantly receiving and transmitting the light of the source, supporting life in their being and in all planes. If they are called to reincarnate light from their current astral existence will enter a physical space of creation. If they had many reincarnations on Earth, it is possible to remember aspects of them for guidance and learning. All lifetimes are stored on Earth's being like memories and you can access them in order to support your current lifetime on the planet.

—--

Question

I have a question about my purpose. I anchor the light daily into Mother Earth and shine and spread my light to all. I take care of the critters, and grow food. I volunteer. Take classes like yoga, Tai Chi, meditation, qigong besides dancing but I feel there's more or am I missing something???? Thank you for taking the time to help guide.

Answer

You have many beautiful gifts and clarity to experience them in your everyday life as well as the ability to share them with others. See all this as a phase of growth and you are now getting ready to move into a new phase. You are opening yourself to experience an inner flow that will reach, strengthen and unite all parts of your being. All activities, gifts, intentions, communications, and exchanges are not going to be experienced as separate parts of you but they are all branches of your true path and purpose.

You may ask: what do I have to do to experience this new cycle of growth? Go deeper into your being, experience peace, connect to your truth, and focus on the greatness and beauty of your being. Everything that you do, even breathing, should take you deep into the core of your being and connect you to the greatness that you are. In this new phase of growth, you will disconnect from the influence of the mind. Often people are looking after their bodies and are involved in other wonderful activities but still are not fully satisfied because the mind interferes. The fear of having to do something in a certain way, the worry that what you do may not be appreciated, the need to know the outcome of all actions are only some of the restrictions that separate you from your true greatness. In the new phase of growth, you will free yourself from the mind, you will dive into the pool of greatness and you will follow the powerful and effortless flow within.

Question

I have a question. What is light language and why do humans tend to corrupt everything? Thank you!

Answer

All beings in all planes are able to communicate by sharing light/energy. This is the most powerful way of communication because it has many qualities such as healing, clarity, opportunities for growth, allowing the cosmic light to be transmitted, supporting collective growth, receiving guidance and much more. Human beings have the ability to communicate energetically but they are not conscious of it. In their conscious state, they often block this ability as they focus on thinking, analyzing, coming to conclusions and expressing all this through language which is a form of communication invented by the mind. If people claim that they are using light language and this is another invention of the mind then energy is not being shared. There are people who claim that they use light language and they still trigger the mind and affect emotions. Energetic communication can be experienced when people are in a state of peace, emptying their minds and experiencing the abilities of their energy field.

When human beings are in a confused state, going on a diversion, they are not aware of their true path; they go against their path and move away from their life purpose. In this great confusion, human beings experience an illusionary reality of survival and completely ignore the abundance of their true path. They may seem to go against others, to be corrupted, deceitful and to want to manipulate but all these are signs of the great confusion in them that is blocking them from experiencing their true state: an effortless flow of joy, creation, connection and growth. Destructive behaviour shows the reality that human beings experience and its limitations.

Question

I would like you to write a system for nourishing ourselves with the right food that we take because that has a lot to do with our health.

Answer

There are a number of steps we can take to support our wellbeing through nourishment. The first step is the observation of our current patterns and a deep purification from destructive habits. Observe your eating and wellbeing patterns:

When do you eat during your day? Do you follow the breakfast-lunch-dinner pattern or perhaps you have a different pattern? How much do you eat? What type of food is attractive to you and why? What is your motivation when you eat? Do you eat with others and how does this affect your eating patterns? Are you in a hurry, working all day long and how is this affecting your eating habits? Is artificiality and consumerism affecting the way you nourish yourself? Are you addicted to unhealthy patterns? If you follow certain patterns, where did they come from? Are they part of your conditioning? Are they supporting fear or limitation in your life?

These are just some questions that you should try to answer by observing yourself. This will bring lots of truths to the surface as to why people find it hard to understand their body and nourish it in the proper way.

Artificial lifestyles are affecting most human beings. They block them from loving and nourishing their body or they discourage them from being connected with their truth and their natural ability to nourish themselves. When you are able to see how artificiality is affecting you, you have started your purification process.

The next step is to empty yourself. Empty yourself from the old patterns, beliefs, fears and limitations about food. Stop with addictions, unhealthy food habits, overeating, not hydrating yourself enough, not taking the time to cook a balanced and nutritional meal. Create a blank canvas and slowly fill it with nourishment that is related to your body. Simplify the way you nourish your body, create it yourself and find joy in it.

Your nutrition is an important ritual to help you empower your connection with Earth. All the nourishment that you need comes directly from her. If you accept this truth, you are not only going to change your eating patterns but also your lifestyle experience.

—--

Question

It has been said that to know one's purpose in life and connect to true self which is a reflection of the higher self, one may need to free one's self from illusions and distortions. The question is: we were born with a conscience, not with religion. This is because as we grow up and as our senses develop we gain consciousness of religion, education, etc. that were introduced to us as part of illusions... distortions from society.

To free oneself from these illusions and distortions, as practical steps can we assume the position of our former state when we are not conscious of ourselves?

And what is my purpose and path in this lifetime?

Answer

Most beings on Earth exist in a hypnotic state. They can be easily manipulated, brainwashed, and have no understanding of their true self and purpose. Your challenge is to wake up and connect to your truth. Everybody can achieve it if this is your true intention. Your whole being should express the wish to communicate to the true-self. For this to happen you may have to change your lifestyle, your values, your understanding, and the way you experience life. When this happens you will feel an illusion trying to drag you back in. You will experience people's opposition, criticism, negativity; you may feel weak and confused. This is how illusion attacks when one tries to escape and often the person is brought back in and tied up.

You have to be strong; say no and step out of it. Soon you will realize that your true life is starting now and you are in control of your growth. You will realize that you have great power and knowledge of the cosmos. You can connect to your astral body and receive light from astral beings that are here to guide you and support you. You will have a life of happiness and all your connections with other beings will experience this with you.

You want me to give you advice as to how you can be free from illusion. Look at what is obviously an expression of the illusion and disconnect yourself from it (education, religion, government). Then you look even further looking at all social structures around you such as social success, lifestyle, work, human relationships, ideas, and beliefs, and try to understand how they are linked to the illusion. Then look at your own life and clear all distortion and blockages that keep you in a lower vibration. This process may take a while; you have to be persistent and patient. When you can connect to your true self you will be able to understand your purpose and naturally, you will be disconnected from illusion.

Question

I wanted to know if my fragmentations will be made whole in this lifetime. Am I carrying these from past reincarnations? Do these imbed my progress to complete my work for this project? Do we design our lives before coming here to Earth? Those fragmentations have caused me the inability to have lasting relationships, which I don't have the ability to correct. Will I be able to, or is this part of the plan and I am yet to understand the reason?

Thank you. I am trying to figure out what my true purpose is, and why such disconnects get thus far.

Answer

All beings on Earth suffer from fragmentation. Your astral body has a very different growth than what you experience on the physical plane. You were created to connect to growth that is taking place in the astral plane and this way you can receive light and guidance in the physical plane. All beings on Earth should know their purpose and be familiar with tools to help them fulfill their purpose.

People who are suffering from fragmentation find it very hard to see the truth. They are easily manipulated and voluntarily give their powers away to become a much lower being than they truly are. If you are aware of your fragmentation, you have already made a great step toward freedom. Now you have to focus on the truth and discard anything that is not true. You have to be fearless, strong, and try to keep your eyes and ears open at all times and never give up because the truth is the only way for you to become whole. When you know your true self many changes will happen: you will start seeing life differently, all the pieces will come together and everything will make sense. You will be clear as to where you are going and what you want to achieve. You will enjoy a balanced existence and you will inspire others to have a balanced life.

—--

Question

Can Thoth tell us what progress is being made to restore Earth's correct mental outlook?

Answer

Earth is going through a long transformation and if it is not interrupted, she is going to experience a new cycle of growth. Distortion is affecting many people on Earth. Global economy, politics and culture are created to disconnect human beings from Earth, their purpose and the connection to the cosmos. There are human beings who are becoming aware of this truth but they still exist in the bubble of illusion.

There is no true energetic balance between different parts of the planet or even within the human being. On the other hand, an increasing number of human beings understand the importance of connecting to Earth and looking for truth within their being. If you want to help Earth go through her transformation you have to heal yourself and connect to the cosmic light. If you transform into your true self, you are supporting Earth, becoming a receiver and transmitter of light.

—---

Question

I am wondering if you have any specifics to help us humans to receive the light and transmit it effectively for example cleansing our bodies, grounding, walking barefoot, having a specific diet or practices that enhance the process?

Answer

There is a lot of advice out there as to how people can experience wellbeing, cleanse their bodies, stay grounded and other important practices that bring balance to their being. Most of these practices are coming to people through their minds not through their whole being.

People are creating a maze with all different choices/advice and they are still confused and in an imbalanced state. Do not focus on your mind if you want to connect to the truth in you. Connect and communicate directly with your physical body if you want to experience healing. Connect to Earth's energies and make it a permanent state if you wish to be grounded. Understand the importance of this connection through your growth. Create bridges from within and let them expand. This will show you that you are not following advice but you are following your truth and purpose.

Question

Is fasting good for your body? I have practised it a little here and there. When I fast for 1-2 days I feel very clear minded and it feels like my body is experiencing something good. I have read how it regenerates cells among other things and how the medical industry will not conduct proper research on fasting.

Answer

Human's way of consuming food that is available to them is very problematic. People who are able to grow the food they eat, they truly nourish their being with food that is alive. This is a way to connect to Earth and receive her energy. When you start consuming fresh fruit and vegetables you are eating patterns will change. The combination of what you eat is also important as well as when you eat it. Most human beings are eating often but they feel constantly hungry.

They do not realize that their food makes them tired and unsatisfied. Eating is a great way to connect to your being and understand its function and ways of growth. When you eat polluted food, you bring imbalance to your body that often leads to disease. Human beings should grow their own food and eat what they produce, connecting to Earth and bringing balance to their body.

If you are not able to produce your own food at this moment, a step forward will be to pick the fruit and vegetables that are grown locally and have what you call "fasting". Limiting your food intake, preparing raw meals and juices should be your everyday diet. This will help you purify your body and also disconnect you from the need of consumption, the fear of survival and the greed that brings destruction to the planet. If you are able to fast for a few days you will experience a feeling of peace and you will be able to disconnect from artificiality and illusions. Your connection to your being will be stronger and the energies of Earth will be flowing in you and nourish you.

Question

What happens in my dreams? They are very ethereal and astral for me and I rarely get to have recall but feel subconscious activity going on all day afterward usually.

Answer

In your dreams, you are able to connect to either the astral plane and connect to your astral body for healing and growth or you may be connecting to your guides that exist in higher planes for guidance and healing. There are some human beings that have the ability to fully disconnect from imbalances and distortions when they enter their sleeping state and this is a great opportunity to connect to your astral body or your guides and receive the high light of creation. Your guides want to remind you about the divine plan of this reincarnation, to help you disconnect from distortion and go on diversions. They also want you to bring the cosmic light to Earth and humanity, nourishing the people around you and support their growth. The light that you are receiving is trying to find its way to your mind and being and becoming your everyday reality. So instead of standing at the crossroads, you should follow the path of your purpose and focus on your growth and the growth of others.

Question

There is much information about chakras becoming blocked and ways to unblock them. Is this an illusion?

Answer

It is illusionary to focus on your chakras and ignore your whole being. Your chakras are gates within your being that allow the energy to flow and heal the imbalances that you may carry; guide you to your purpose; connect you to Earth. Most of the imbalances do not affect the chakras but they exist in the mind, your aura or parts of your being that are in separation from the truth that you carry. You receive the light in order to heal all imbalances and transform your being. Your whole being should experience transformation and this will allow it to be guided to your purpose. This way you fight distortion and fragmentation and you experience unity with the cosmos and Earth.

Question

What would help or benefit me to find inner stillness and peace again?

Answer

There are parts of you that have remained hidden and you can experience absolute peace when you connect to your whole being. See your being as a house of many rooms. Only when you are able to open all the doors, observe and experience all parts of your house will you be able to use it effectively for comfortable living and wellbeing. Do not be afraid to enter all the rooms and discover your special abilities, the truth and growth that you carry, the light that can help you transform into a perfect receiver and transmitter of cosmic light on Earth. When you know yourself you will enter a state of peace and you will start to grow.

Question

Talking about my purpose in life, how do I know what I am doing is according to this purpose?

Answer

People on Earth are very confused. One of the main reasons for this is their fragmentation. They want to know their purpose but they live their lives according to people's expectations and demands. This is a schism which brings confusion and uncertainty. If you are able to block everything that is not your true-self and distance yourself from the ideals of others, then you will instantly know what your purpose is and you will follow your purpose because it is the only truth. Truth feeds you because it is the light that has created you. When you know your truth you will never go back to illusion; you will never have questions and you will live in harmony with everything that exists. You have reincarnated to prove that even in the deepest fog you can find your way. This is your challenge.

Question

The star gates which were created by beings can be found in secret locations in the physical plane as well as in different planes which mirror the physical Earth.

The different planes that Thoth speaks of, what are these?

Answer

The cosmos exists in unity and the cosmic light that brings life to all, connects all different planes. The astral plane is a cosmic laboratory of creation. It is the home of all beings as you can all grow according to cosmic laws and see your connection with the source as your purpose. There are many planes and sub-planes; some of them support beings to have a unique lesson or a preparation, moving towards the astral plane and other planes that have a higher vibration than the astral plane. They are created to support the light of the source created in the cosmos. Earth exists in a low vibrational plane that has a number of layers. At the end of this reincarnation, the essence of a human being will go through purification in order to go through the different layers and finally reconnect to the astral body and the astral plane.

—--

Question

Was the reptilian race the first one on planet Earth before humanity? How was humanity created? Were there multiple seedings of the human race on Earth? Is the human race a slave race to the giant/reptilian races? Was the human race reduced to a very limited state of being through genetic manipulation and reduction in their DNA info to 2 strands? Is the human race border line operating as artificial intelligence? Are there humans that cannot connect to the source/field of consciousness/higher-self because their system is shut?

Answer

During the golden era, Earth created beings with unique body structure, a mixture of plant, animal, humanoid, rock formations or water. All these beings grew and transformed on the planet, nourished themselves with the energies and saw themselves as part of Earth's body. These beings experienced the high light of the golden era, they were aware of Earth's intention, growth and purpose and co-created with her, supporting the expansion of Earth's physical body.

When the astral visitors came to Earth, they brought distorted energies that affected the balance and harmony experienced by Earth beings. The visitors wanted to loot, colonize and make wars in order to keep their control. Earth allowed all her creations that existed on the surface to move to the inner parts and this way isolated the visitors on the surface of the planet. They were not able to enter the inner parts and the Earth beings were able to continue their existence there and experience the golden era.

Reptilian-looking beings were some of the Earth beings that moved to the inner parts of the Earth. A great schism separated the inner parts that continued to grow in the energies of the golden era and the surface of the Earth where visitors came and went and groups of them stayed and made it their home.

Astral beings started to reincarnate on the surface of the Earth to heal the schism and Earth got involved in forming their physical body. Over the many cycles of growth, Earth created new species on the surface of the planet whose existence was affected by low vibrations. The human race is not a slave race to the giant/reptilian races. These are illusions carried by human beings on the surface due to the fear of survival and death; this is a distortion. The human race was not reduced to a very limited state of being through genetic manipulation and reduction in their DNA info to 2 strands. The human beings on the surface went through many fear/survival as well as growth cycles having a life in a low vibrational space. Even though they still experience upheavals, human beings are slowly moving towards a higher vibrational state of existence. Humans on the surface of the Earth may have mechanical lifestyles and experience life through patterns but the true purpose of their existence is to receive and transmit light and therefore heal the schisms on Earth. Human beings are given many opportunities to fulfil their purpose and because of their free will, they can experience it if they chose it.

Question

The source's intentions are beyond our perception? Do we even get a glimpse? Are we just supposed to play our part? Do we connect to the source through the Gods?

Answer

Human beings or any other being in the cosmos are not designed to understand the intention of our source but they are designed to experience it. This can be achieved by connecting to your truth and becoming the creator of your life, following the path of growth. Human beings have to focus on their own path if they wish to connect to the cosmos that is the creation of our source. Do not let the river of confusion and limitation take you away from connecting to your truth and become a perfect transmitter and receiver of cosmic light. People's minds are full of thoughts that are not supporting their purification, growth and creation. When you disconnect from illusionary thinking and acting then you will be able to find the path of your purpose and experience cosmic creation on Earth.

Question

How do I know the difference between guidance from my higher self and the ego? I hear "intuition" often, but I have a hard time discerning if the first thing that comes to me is true intuition of my ego telling me what I want to hear.

Answer

Human beings are affected by many voices and it happens that when you are strongly connected to the illusion that the voice of your ego is the loudest. If you are looking for clarity you have to find your way to your true self and this can be done by examining and testing all the information that comes to you. The voice of the ego often talks to you about survival, fear, negativity, short-lived success which is often linked to competition and scheming. The voice of the ego will never tell you the truth about your current situation; you find yourself often looking at the pyramid trying to go up the steps and receive the illusionary prizes. If the ego does not encourage you to go up the steps of the pyramid then it is going to terrorize you with the idea of suffering, fear and disability. The voice of ego will never bring you peace and only when you are in peace you are connected to truth. If you are in doubt try to enter a space of peace, and see your body as a multidimensional being receiving and transmitting cosmic energy. Disconnect from your illusionary state to enter the cosmic state and then see yourself reincarnated on Earth to fulfil a unique purpose. In this state, you will be able to connect to truth and the voice of the ego will fade away.

Question:

We are products of our environment and most go through life just trying to survive until it is over. This is the expectation of society. However, those who know there is more and who seek to find the truth about the nature of our existence will become open channels for cosmic truth from the gods. They cannot force us (due to free will) yet they do not judge. Those who make this connection and become messengers should spread it to others as well. I'm assuming the expectation isn't only to preach the message, correct? People are not always receptive and are often hostile if you speak of spiritual matters.

Answer

First, you have to allow the light to go through you, clear all imbalances, restore you to a perfect state and clear your path of growth. When this happens you will know how to bring the light of the cosmos to Earth. Different people have different tools and different skills to help them express the light and share it with others. There is no doubt receiving and transmitting light is part of your purpose because it is connected to cosmic growth. When you have clarity and you are able to recognize your tools and skills then you will be able, in a unique way, to share the light with others. For the time being, do not be afraid to share your passion for enlightenment with others because this will bring clarity.

Question

I see myself trying to get in touch with myself and live an authentic, purposeful life, which I find very challenging. Your videos and articles are inspiring, although I caution myself from jumping too quickly into something. Where do you recommend going next?

Answer

Thank you for joining this space of truth. First, you need to ask yourself what you mean by the phrase "trying to live with yourself." How do you connect to yourself and what is the true purpose of this connection? How far away are you from illusion and what do you do to help and inspire others to find their own paths? Many people on Earth try to wake up but they find it a challenging task and sometimes misleading. You think you are awake but you still maintain old blockages. You think you are following your path but you are still suffering from insecurities and fear. I can show you the way to truth and it is a clear path, easy to find and easy to follow: connect to everything that is true in you and disconnect from all artificialities, insecurities and illusionary realities. Observe your life and find out what gives you true power to create and help others. It may be certain qualities, abilities, skills, or understanding that you have. These qualities can help you experience true life and when you are free and open to cosmic light you will be powerful and this power will be directed to others who are waiting to be free too. Follow the path of truth, this is the only way.

Question

Are crystals a good way to connect with some of these energies from the inner Earth?

Answer

I know that human beings are attracted to crystals because they remind them of the golden era when giant crystals were created on Earth to receive light and transmit it to the planet. During the golden era, there were mountains of crystals scattered around the planet, crystals were everywhere in all different shapes and sizes and what you have right now is just rocks and stones. Those crystal formations were not made by human beings but they were created by Earth and the cosmic light to support her growth. There were her receivers and transmitters of light, Later on, these crystals were destroyed or looted by the alien races that came to Earth.

The energy of the stones that people can have on Earth right now is only a fraction of the ones that existed in the golden era. Also, crystals are receiving the low energies, the distortion, and the limitation that human beings carry and they transmit that.

If you want to have stones and you want to use them to help you connect to Earth's growth and golden era, they have to be stored underground, and when they are used you need to have a clear and pure intention regarding their use. Crystals and stones that are placed constantly in a room, have no healing qualities and it is also possible that they may transmit distortion.

Question

What planet did humans originate from?

Answer

Many astral beings that belonged to different races, visited Earth from the time of her Golden era to the present times. Some of these races did not make Earth their permanent home on Earth and others created civilisations that expanded not only on the surface but also in the inner parts of the Earth. The planet went through several transformations including what you call catastrophic changes, disasters and mass extinction of a number of species that lived on the planet. Right now there is a distinction between animals and humanoid beings and this was the result of the changes of the planet and the low vibration of Earth. You also have certain races such as black African, caucasian and so on and are related to different astral races that existed on Earth before Earth's transformation. The races known to you are the humanoids of Earth who were isolated and created civilisations similar to what is described in your books about prehistoric times. Earth's changes and transformations affected all beings; some became extinct and others reappeared on Earth having a different form, consciousness and light.

Question

I have always been fascinated with different creatures that I read about and some have been considered "myths" but I have wondered if that is really the truth. For example, were dragons, wyverns, or chimaera purely fictional? What about spirits in nature like faeries, gnomes or perhaps mermaids? Also, does such a thing exist as the dead rising like zombies, ghouls or vampires? How about werewolves? Was that something false as well? Thank you

Answer

The animals and creatures that can be visible on Earth right now are only a small percentage of what existed on Earth thousands of years ago. If you were able to look back at Earth's history from the golden era to the present time, you could see many phases of transformation affecting Earth's creation. During the golden era, living beings had high-dimensional bodies that had direct communication with their astral body. Those beings were high receivers and transmitters of light and were created to support Earth, becoming a powerful creator of life. Your physicality and senses will not be able to detect these beings because of your restriction to experience life beyond your third dimension. Earth's creation was transformed physically and energetically following Earth's vibrational changes. Those changes were marked by a series of temporary terminations of life on Earth and the beginning of a new cycle of evolution. Many of the creatures that you read about in your books have existed on the planet. Some of them still exist but they are not able to be perceived by human beings. They are still working with Earth receiving and transmitting light and they want to support humanity reconnecting to Earth and understand their purpose which is connecting to the cosmic light and healing the planet and her creation.

Question

Are there some flora and fauna that are not native to Earth that exists on the planet?

Answer

Everything that exists on Planet Earth is created by Earth. And this can be explained by looking at each planet's ability to create life. It will be useless trying to plant seeds that are designed to connect to Earth's energies, on Mars. Similarly, you will not want to go for a walk in the moon's atmosphere without protection and necessary equipment that will re-connect you to Earth's ability to create.

Question

Can you tell me about medicine; how to practise medicine within the "social structure", but without conforming to the standards of society...in other words...how to stay close to true healing while having to go through mainstream medical training.

Answer

Civilized life means an artificial life: Civilized people, living in a civilized manner and eating civilized foods, can not, in the very nature of things, have a truly healthy colon. Health & Sickness both have their roots in the Colon." I would like to draw your attention to another health hazard. Fever-fighting drugs are not wise to take and this shows again the naivety and ignorance of people to listen to the lies and deceit of doctors who are the slaves and workers for big pharma. People should focus on preventing disease instead of trying to cure the symptom of the disease. It is hilarious to see the representatives of pharmaceutical companies such as scientists and doctors trying to find ways to heal a physical body with chemicals.

Mainstream medical training is designed and controlled by organisations that want to observe human life and try to imitate it in artificial life forms. If you study medicine you support these organisations because you can not be independent of them. They control all treatments and medical substances. There are cases that humanity has benefited from certain medical practices and there are ways to heal patients by following western medicine. You have to ask yourself what you want to achieve. Are you concerned with healing and giving the freedom to a patient to achieve that? Do you prefer to go through medical school and try to heal people while being part of a vast industry of fear and control? Perhaps you can study western medicine as well as other healing modalities and try to combine them in a unique way. At this point, I want to ask you what is your path, what were your tools and what is your intention? If you know the answer to these questions then you will know what path to take.

Question

Lately, I find that I must disassociate myself from people, because they are either toxic, or a distraction by numerous means, such as drama.

In some cases, these are family members, and I wonder how to balance family obligations with my need to focus on my own growth and well-being. It seems that there is an equal force that wants us to fail, and the more we work on ourselves, the more obstacles it seems one must overcome. Does Thoth have any words of advice?

Answer

People who are close to you need to be treated with kindness and understanding. Being on your path and trying to bring clarity to your life does not mean that you have to cut your ties with the people who are genuinely connected to you even if your understanding and perception of the cosmos are very different from theirs. You can enjoy being with people that have a different path from you. What is important is that you both genuinely care for each other and you are willing to support each other with your light. Trying to convince people about your understanding of life with words and opposition will make you both vulnerable and your light will not be shared so it will become weak. When you are able to see yourself as a free and pure being with unlimited opportunities you will be guided by your light. Your light will help you to connect to people around you and create meaningful relationships as well as experience a balanced life. If you are experiencing obstacles on your way to growth this means that you have not yet met your true- self and you are still influenced by the illusion which is blocking your way. Challenge yourself; try to connect to your true self away from all artificiality. This is your path and it is open.

Question

While there seems to be a life cycle to solar systems, and we have evidence of stars dying out and planets drifting away, or being consumed by supernovas, or being smashed by asteroids, how can it be that the Earth is eternal?

Answer

Human beings have physical bodies; planets have physical bodies too. A physical body of a human being has a short life cycle and at the end of this cycle, the being will return to the astral plane and continue to grow and evolve. Astral growth is eternal and limitless. Planets have much longer life cycles and go through many transformations. Human beings are not able to know all of Earth's transformations because they have not experienced them; they did not grow with Earth. If Earth loses her physical body will not affect human beings directly. If this happens human beings will stop reincarnating on Earth. It may be that planets have to lose their physicality similarly to human beings, enter a non-physical vibrational

223

state and start existing as an astral body. We talk about Earth being eternal; this is related to her ability to create life and give opportunities to astral beings to reincarnate and experience physicality. Earth produces life, creates receivers and transmitters of cosmic light and allows energies to create bridges with other cosmic life. She is offering a gift of growth and this makes her a creator.

—--

Question

Some people may ask how we can search for our life path without any support or guidance; it is natural that we are going to get lost because we don't know either the final destination or the route to it.

Answer

People on Earth have a great deal of support and guidance coming to them from the astral plane but they choose not to communicate with their spiritual guides. Everything that is pure in you, I call it diaphanous, you hide away, you dismiss it, you disconnect from it. If you wish to find your path don't look at the sparkling, inviting and deceiving mind structures. Simply look inside yourself and find this sacred part of you, your purity, and make it your guide. Be diaphanous, exist and live as a diaphanous being.

—--

Question

I want to ask Thoth about variation in the universe. Is the human template a common form in the universe?

Answer

If you want an answer to this question you should look at all the different trees and their leaves. For beings who exist on low vibrational planets that have a growth that is similar to Earth's growth, you will find beings who look very similar to human beings: perhaps a different colour, different height or it may be a difference in the formation of some body parts. There are also planets that have the same vibration as Earth but the beings who exist there look different from the Earthlings because they live underground or they were exposed to some major disaster. In higher realms beings consist of energy and have no physicality. There are also realms where beings can be recognised by the aura that surrounds their limited physicality. As you can see there are many variations but there are also similarities: their ability to grow, their connection to the cosmic light and the source and their ability to support cosmic growth.

Question

Why do we have to forget our past lives if we live in an infinite creation system?

Answer

Human beings on Earth are connected to the light of the cosmos. This is a natural law and it is also a cosmic law. The astral being that is going to be reincarnated on Earth is aware of its past reincarnations, the lessons that need to be learned and the divine plan of the reincarnation. When the being is in the womb, it is still astral energy that is allowing the physical body to be created. The physical body is the vehicle to help the being experience life on Earth.

When the baby is born it is trying to balance the astral and the physical existence. It is still experiencing a connection to the astral plane and it is still aware of the divine plan of this reincarnation. Earth's third-dimensional reality weakens a being's ability to connect to the astral plane but the biggest obstacle is growing up among beings that have completely disconnected themselves from their astral growth and furthermore the social systems that support illusionary beliefs and create distortion in people's minds.

Young children are forced to think of their future role in society. They are programmed to accept illusion as truth and completely ignore their purpose and the divine plan of their reincarnation even if they decide to connect to their true self at some point in their lives, they will have a hard time purifying themselves from countless layers of illusion, distortion and artificiality that have affected them over the years. Freedom and truth are stages of growth that not many people experience on Earth. If you connect to them and you allow them to guide you, you will connect to your true self and purify your imbalances. Knowing the divine plan of your reincarnation is your right and duty. You are all able to fulfil your purpose because the obstacles that stop you are illusionary and are not part of your divine plan. Allow truth to enter your house and be your guide and best friend. Then freedom will follow.

Question

The lower spirits, the manipulators..Is there any potential for rebirth through purification for them?

Answer

All beings have to go through purification in order to return to the astral plane and continue with their growth. This happens at the end of a reincarnation or any cycle of growth. The period of purification is not the same for all beings. For some, purification is just an assessment of their achievements and for other beings, it is a very long process of relearning and cleansing imbalances. There are also beings who remain in a lower non-physical state because they are not able to grow. However, the essence of all beings in the cosmos aims to connect to the source and therefore growth and evolution are available to all.

Question

Can you comment on the origin of the asteroid field between Mars and Jupiter?

Answer

Mars and Jupiter are not from the same family of planets. They are very different and have different purposes. Mars was inhabited by different humanoid races and it was a low vibrational planet and the home of energetically lower beings and their civilisations. There were areas on Mars that resembled Earth but there were also lands of desolation because of great planetary wars that took place there. What took place on Mars is taking place right now on Earth; the obsession of destruction and going against natural law has caused the termination and distinction of many forms of life. There is one difference between Earth and Mars and this is that Earth is a Goddess planet and is connected directly to the Source. Jupiter is a high vibrational planet and human beings will never be able to reach all its different dimensions.

—————-------------------------------------

Question

Can you please speak more about the young children incarnated on Earth at this time and how best to guide them?

Answer

Children should be free to explore life on Earth. The more freedom they have to experience life, be their true-self, connect to physical and non-physical beings and allow them to see life being part of a cosmic creation without boundaries the more grounded they will become. Allow your children to teach you, connect to them energetically and try not to focus on artificiality or illusion. Children can connect to the astral plane but they can also be affected by illusion if they are exposed to it. You should free yourself from illusion and the children will be able to connect to your purity and help you grow with them. Show them what is most precious and beautiful for you and let them feed from it. Children always give you back what you have given them.

Vocabulary

Astral body is an extension of your physical body and occupies a great area of energetic fields called the astral plane. The astral body is in constant growth, connecting to the highlight of the cosmos and following the cosmic laws in order to receive and transmit the high light of the cosmos. Having a physical form does not restrict you from connecting to your astral body and becoming part of the growth and evolution that takes place there. Connecting to your truth and purpose and going through the process of purification, transformation and growth, you are allowing constant connection and communication between your physical and astral body.

Astral core created by the intention of the source. It supported the creation of the astral plane and its sub-planes. The astral core went through many transformations and with the support of the cosmic light, it continued to grow and expand within the being of the source. The communication between the light and the core was clear and direct and supported countless transformations and the creation of a new divine plan. Energy fields were created by the light to offer support and more opportunities for the core's expansion. The source created a divine plan about the creation of the astral plane with its subplanes, guided by cosmic laws. The astral plane has the ability to expand limitlessly and always remain an extension of the source.

Astral plane is the true home of all beings. In the astral plane, all physical beings lose their physicality and exist in their pure form which is their light. The astral plane is a place of transformation and growth. It is the home of all beings; it is the home of all creation. Beings have their own purpose and their own plan for growth and this is why the astral plane is divided into many sub-planes which have different frequency levels. Beings are not left on their own to seek truth and growth but they are connected to many other beings that have the same frequency as them; they connect to higher beings who are their guides and lower beings that are supported by them. In the astral plane, there is no destruction, all beings have clarity and therefore they experience their plan of growth.

In this state you receive guidance from your higher self and divine intervention from your creation code. Your astral body is aware of your purpose and growth cycles; cosmic truth and wisdom go through the astral body in the form of energy and this is why it is in a process of constant purification and transformation.

Aura is an electromagnetic field that surrounds all physical bodies and allows them to receive and transmit energy. Your aura helps you communicate energetically, supports the body to function and stay balanced, staying grounded and connecting to the cosmos and astral body. Distortion and fragmentation can affect the aura as well as the physical body.

Code of Creation (creation code) is a "geometric" code that is used to create and maintain life. Our source is always within us; we all carry the creation code which is a living being and is affected by our consciousness, the light that we possess and the way we use it. The unity that exists in the cosmos is contained in the light of our creator and is spread to the creation through our creation code. The creation code can be understood as the intention of the source to create life. All beings are connected to the source because every part of their being in all planes is connected to the creation code.

All beings that exist in all planes are created in the astral plane and therefore they have an astral body that is in constant transformation and growth. The guide of the astral body is the higher self. The higher self is aware of all transformation and growth, all connections, duties and paths that the astral body can experience. The higher self supports the astral body to follow the cosmic laws, experience unity with the cosmos, receive and transmit light and move closer to the source by supporting growth in all planes.

The creation code is the high seed of all beings and it exists with the source. All beings are able to connect to their creation code. The gods do not have access to the creation code but they do connect to the higher self. The creation code cannot be altered; the source creates through the gods using cosmic light and then the gods become the source's creative tool.

Consciousness contains the "highlights" of one's growth and has two main uses: one is to record, maintain and stabilize one's growth and the second is to be used as a guide for other entities who wish to work with this person in the astral or physical plane. There is also a collective consciousness which some people confuse with the beliefs of certain social groups. Collective is the consciousness of Earth and its reflection on all beings that live on the planet. This is when a unit of growth connects with other units of growth that are affected by the same electromagnetic fields.

Cosmic laws are a reflection of the natural laws which exist on Earth. All planes are regulated by cosmic laws. When these cosmic laws are not followed we have high levels of distortion and imbalances similar to what Earth is experiencing right now. Enlightenment is the result of our connection and understanding of cosmic laws. Everything we seek is waiting for us if we connect to the cosmos and act accordingly. Another cosmic law is the unity of all creation brings energy, balance, and strength to receivers and transmitters and more opportunity for further growth.

Cosmic light is the light of our source which spreads to all creation. Its purpose is to offer life, growth and guidance and connect all creation. High creator gods have the ability to connect to the light of the creator to create life. Gods are not in control of this high creative force, they do not fully understand how it works and furthermore, they cannot reproduce it. Instead, the light creates through them. When the High Light passes information from the creation code, the form of a being first develops in the astral plane. In the physical plane, beings learn to experience life through the five senses or the limitations of a physical body. Beings that experience an astral existence simultaneously with their physical reality are able to acquire knowledge leading to a new cycle of growth.

Clarity is a clear understanding of one's purpose. Having clarity you are able to see your path and create all the necessary circumstances to help you achieve your goal. Clarity is a divine tool given to all beings to enable them to communicate with their astral body and connect them to their purpose. Clarity can be achieved if we simply look deep inside ourselves, connect to our purity, and make it our guide.

Distortion is an energetic imbalance that has affected Earth and her creation and is caused by the trauma of Earth, the end of her golden era and her inability to cope as a high creator. The third-dimensional reality, with its lower vibration, is the ideal space for distortion to grow and expand. As a result, people living in a constant hypnotic state of illusion and stagnation disconnected from the purpose and divine plan.

Divine light is a powerful creative force in the cosmos created by the source. The unity of the divine and cosmic light supported the bond between the source and its cosmic creation and this is how life was maintained and grew in the astral plane. The cosmic light is a pure and powerful cosmic force that creates life in all planes and the divine light is a tool of precision that supports cosmic laws, transformations, movement, growth and connection between all beings and planes. Astral beings are created by cosmic light and divine light and are part of energy fields that support the expansion of the astral plane and the creation of sub-planes.

Divine plan is a set of instructions that are created by the source and support creation in all planes. The divine plan initiates a new cycle of growth and is transfered by the cosmic light to all living beings. Astral beings that reincarnate on Earth are aware of their purpose and divine plan, unique abilities leading to an effortless life of receiving and transmitting light, growth, and transformation. The divine plan exists in the core of a being and can support the creation of a life path and the being's special abilities.

Duality is the separation of self from all that exists. When children start to become aware of society's structures, they start to lose their ability to experience unity. The focus in their lives will be indoctrination, focusing on the mind-logic-limitation and being part of a life of duality, fragmentation and non-growth. There is always a fight of opposites which is the cause of fragmentation and illusion. If you wish to evolve beyond duality, you have to disconnect from the idea of opposites. In nature there is no fight against two elements, there is only a union of the elements, bringing new life.

Enlightenment is not our final destination in our quest for growth but is just a single step towards gnosis. Masters have to take many steps of enlightenment in order to comprehend just a small piece of the vastness of the cosmos. Becoming receivers and transmitters of light, you allow the cosmic flow to enter humanity and Earth.

Essence is the presence of the High Source which nobody can destroy or alter. Our growth depends on our ability to create and for this to happen we have to recognize and understand our essence and our creation code. The essence of Earth, in the physical plane, can be described as the golden era, a time of high creation.

Fragmentation is an imbalance on Earth that can be understood as a separation of self from all that exists. On Earth, beings experience fragmentation that affects inner unity, clarity and disability to connect to their purpose and truth. Fragmentation can affect the connection between humanity and Earth and allow cosmic light to be received and transmitted to all life.

Gnosis is wisdom.

The **Golden Era** was a time of high creation. In the golden era, all beings had a different cycle. Their light was eternal and they were able to be reborn. The colours and the shapes on Earth gave her a high vibration and all creation was connected to this. The cosmic laws ruled Earth's existence and purity was clearly seen and experienced in all beings.

Everything that existed on Earth had to produce light and energy to support the planet's growth. The whole planet was united and went through purification and transformation as a whole being. They received light from the high realms and they transmitted light to support the cosmos. In the golden era, there were many beings that were able to nourish themselves with light. The animal kingdom received nourishment directly from the Earth and other beings on the planet were connected to the light of the cosmos. What you are experiencing in your time, animals eating each other, started to take place when the vibration of Earth became lower. During the golden era, Earth resembled what you now call exotic and tropical nature. Earth was created to have enough resources to feed and nourish all her creations. Plants and animals were fed with the minerals and other nutrients which could be found on Earth as well as the light from the electromagnetic fields of the planet.

Growth is synonymous with life. All living beings have multiple opportunities to transform and grow, receiving and transmitting cosmic light. All of you come on Earth to fulfil your purpose, this means to achieve growth and spread this growth to humanity and Earth. You will be given opportunities to achieve this and the events are recorded in your divine plan. There are people who are going to pollute their beings with artificiality and distortion; this is their choice. They are responsible for their own growth and when they go against their growth, their opportunities diminish. There is a divine plan that shapes a being's existence but human beings with their actions, thoughts and creation can increase or decrease their opportunities for growth.

Higher self is the true essence of a being and exists in a much higher vibration than the astral body. The higher self directs evolution and connects to the astral body when certain light and information are needed for its growth. Everything that exists is really a reflection of a lower or a higher related body. In other words all bodies are reflections of each other.

High Creator has no form, character or attributes. Our High Creator is the perfect representation of life where everything is effortless, whole and limitless. High Gods can only dream to be in this state of absolute perfection, where there is nothing to see and yet everything exists simultaneously. Our High Creator is not a human being; it is a state of the highest growth and the highest consciousness. Our Creator is limitless: its whole creation, everything that exists, it is only a fragment of our source's existence.

Illusion appears as multiple layers of distorted reality that people accept as true. It is highly versatile and being formless can take any temporary form. When human beings receive this temporary form of illusion and accept it as real, they give it life and form which is able to grow and implant in different people. Illusion does not have a form or growth and has the tendency to connect to low self; it becomes part of this person's experience and then quickly needs to spread to others in order to acquire power.

Logos is a vibrational creation tool, a pure reflection of our source, which is given to high gods to create life. Logos is communication between the source and the living being high god and through this connection, the creative intention of the source goes through the lower being who is the creator god and through him/her the source creates.

New Planes consist of multiple subplanes and were created as an extension of the astral plane. The new planes became the home of physical creation and went through many transformations to support physical creation and overall growth and balance. The new planes were also called lower planes because of the low vibration, distortion and imbalances that affected the physical creation.

Pleroma is a separate plane that exists in direct connection with the source. The Pleroma is the highest plane and consists of different energetic layers and subdivisions. It is inhabited by gods and god creators.

Polarity is a division that creates two opposites. This is an imbalance that can be experienced in low vibrational states where the human mind distracts the natural and cosmic processes of a being. Polarity goes against unity and creates obstacles for people to accept, remain in peace or connect to the truth in them.

Purification is a process of cleansing all imbalances, blockages, fears, limitations, and restrictions of illusionary patterns/beliefs/states in order to experience your true abilities,

weaknesses, strengths, talents and skills. The process of purification includes observation, the practice of self-love and acceptance, creating a space of peace, connecting to Earth and the cosmos and allowing truth to guide you to your path.

Purity is this part of you that cannot be affected by any sort of manipulation, fragmentation and distortion. All beings carry purity in them. It is their light, which was given to them when they were created. It is the link between the being, the god and the source. When you follow purity, you are truly happy and satisfied; able to make your greatest contribution in your life and in the life of others; transform yourself and others; have no doubt as to what your purpose is and you will be able to fulfil it.

Purpose of a being is related to the divine plan and the true expression of life. Third-dimensional beings can fulfil their purpose and can experience growth if they are able to clear blockages and imbalances.

Reincarnation offers the opportunity for a being to receive and offer teachings. People reincarnate wherever and whenever there is a need for this to happen. They are beings who have reincarnated many times on Earth and they are other beings who have reincarnated on many other planets, galaxies and universes. For every being, there is a divine plan, a plan of evolution, and this is stored in its creation code and is manifested in its higher self. According to this plan, beings will go through a certain learning process that is tailored specifically for them.

Schism is a severe form of fragmentation that can create strong polarities, imbalances and destruction. Earth's inability to heal herself and her creation led to complete detachment from gods' intervention. When human beings create great schisms in them, they can lose their humanity; they become a different species.

Soul is a great educator and guides beings to their true purpose. It is an aid, helping beings to open up to their astral existence and what lies beyond that. At the beginning of reincarnation, a link is created between the physical and the astral body and when the body dies this link, which is the soul, disconnects from the physical body and goes back to the astral. The soul does not evolve and it is not the purest part of a being as many think.

Transformation is a process of rebirth. When you are in transformation you are able to produce, transmit and receive different energies and use your light to achieve great growth.

True self helps us understand our purpose and our tools. It is important that you safeguard your truth and do not let others pull you into the illusion with their criticism and negativity. Let your light guide you and others; enjoy a balanced life unknown to many and bring this gift to others. People who follow truth have an effortless life because they are balanced and exist to fulfil their purpose. People who are aware of their true-self have nothing to hide and their evolution and growth are guaranteed.

Wormholes and stargates are entrance points on Earth. There are different types of star gates, some of them are divine creations and others were built by beings from other planets who wish to visit Earth. The star gates created by the gods are placed on important points of the Earth's grid and this corresponds to the star gates on different planets and galaxies. These entrances form an energetic shape that works as a magnet for constant energy flow and balance. The star gates which were created by beings can be found in secret locations in the physical plane as well as in different planes which mirror the physical Earth. These star gates connect different geographical points on Earth as well as places on other planets and other dimensions.

There is no higher truth than connecting to your essence, understand your unique abilities and creating the path that will help you fulfil your purpose. There is no higher duty than connecting to the cosmic light, allowing it to bring healing and knowing to your whole being, helping you to exist in unity with Earth and the cosmos. Becoming a receiver of the cosmic light will help you to understand the importance of transmitting the light to others and become a co-creator of life. The healing that you receive is not owned by you; it will support your growth when you are able to transmit it to others. Pure intention opens many doors between the cosmos, Earth and humanity.

Printed and bound by CPI Group (UK) Ltd, Croydon, CR0 4YY